# THE COMPLETE ARCHITECTURE OF BALKRISHNA DOSHI
## RETHINKING MODERNISM FOR THE DEVELOPING WORLD

JAMES STEELE

# THE COMPLETE ARCHITECTURE OF BALKRISHNA DOSHI

## RETHINKING MODERNISM FOR THE DEVELOPING WORLD

WITH 239 ILLUSTRATIONS, 120 IN COLOUR

THAMES AND HUDSON

© 1998 Thames and Hudson Ltd, London

British Library Cataloguing-in-Publication Data
A catalogue record for this book is available from
the British Library

ISBN 0-500-28082-7

Printed and bound by C+C Offset Printing
Company Ltd, Hong Kong

**Above**  Aranya Low-Cost Housing, Indore 1986

**Opposite title page**  Gandhi Labour Institute, Ahmedabad 1984

# Contents

Introduction

## Projects

# INTRODUCTION

**Below and right** Le Corbusier, Courts of Justice, Chandigarh 1955. The sun-screens and main entrance on the western facade are reflected in the water, enhancing the monumental quality of the building.

**Opposite** Le Corbusier, Parliament Building, Chandigarh 1962. The hyperbolic curve of the roughcast concrete sunshade contrasts with the rectilinear screenwall and pierced openings.

# Introduction

*Searching for an Appropriate Indian Architecture:*
*Sources of Influence in History and Culture*

India is hurtling through the invisible envelope that separates a 'developing' from a 'developed' country. Since Independence fifty years ago, the rapid expansion of India's middle class has created an unrivalled level of media attention. Balkrishna V. Doshi's career spans this turbulent period of national growth and change. He is one of the most visionary leaders of a generation who have been searching for a continuous strand in the long history of Indian architecture, as well as a valid means of contemporary interpretation. The official sanctioning of modern architecture by Prime Minister Nehru as the approved national style and symbol of a fresh start after Independence has been a defining factor in Doshi's work. His early association with two of the most influential 'form-givers' in modern architecture, Le Corbusier and Louis Kahn, has made an indelible impression on him and provides the key to a substantial understanding of his approach.

There has been a surprising lack of commentary on Doshi, with only one dedicated study in what amounts to an extended article by William Curtis prior to this analysis. Many commentators other than Curtis identify three distinct stages in his work, beginning with modernist influence in the 1960s and early 1970s, through a search for indigenous Indian models until the mid-1980s, evolving into the current phase of almost primal, mystic studies related to early Buddhist, Hindu

and Islamic models and a complete exclusion of Western influences. Doshi himself has rejected this tripartite staging because he has continually attempted a synthesis, not rejection of Western influences with his own culture.

An attempt to bring this architect's work into register with that of others in the developing world, such as Hassan Fathy in Egypt or Rasem Badran of Jordan, for example, who are often superficially characterized as intractable opponents of the International Style and the homogenization of culture that it is seen to represent, must take this critical difference of synthesis into account. William Curtis has come closer to the mark by recognizing 'the strength and relevance of the import' as well as 'the resilience and cultural depth of the recipient', which makes India a particularly interesting case study in this debate. The modern models contributed by such important architects as Le Corbusier and Kahn have been of such a high calibre that they have established an enduring framework or 'filter' for everything that has followed it.

Balkrishna Doshi has done nothing less than refine and perpetuate the central principles of modern architecture as they relate to the history, climate and diverse cultural mixture of India. Rather than presenting the neat, tripartite evolution from Corbusian rationalism toward proto-Gandhian mysticism, as some

would characterize his increasingly complex *oeuvre*, Doshi's work has consistently revolved around notions of the interrelationship of indoor and outdoor space, an appropriate and honest approach to materials, proper climatic response and the observance of hierarchy and order that have always been present in the best modern architecture and conspicuously absent in poor imitations. It is the 'filter' that Curtis has identified that makes Doshi's interpretations so valuable, since it may offer a more realistic guide for the future in both India and other countries that have experienced a similar path of development. That filter is intricate, since it contains so many closely woven historical, religious and social strands, which make up one of the richest cultures in the world, and its intricacy makes it difficult to analyse.

In speaking of internal and external integration of space, Doshi mentions the need to 'express a cosmic relationship' and insists that aesthetic considerations in design include 'local symbolism and associations'. His most recent work is replete with mythological and visionary allusions reminiscent of the rich story-telling tradition in India; most notable are the tortoises and cobras in the Husain-Doshi Gufa and the crystalline 'caves' in the Bombay Diamond Bourse now under construction. The free-form plan of the Gufa, whose radical departure from carefully ordered structures of

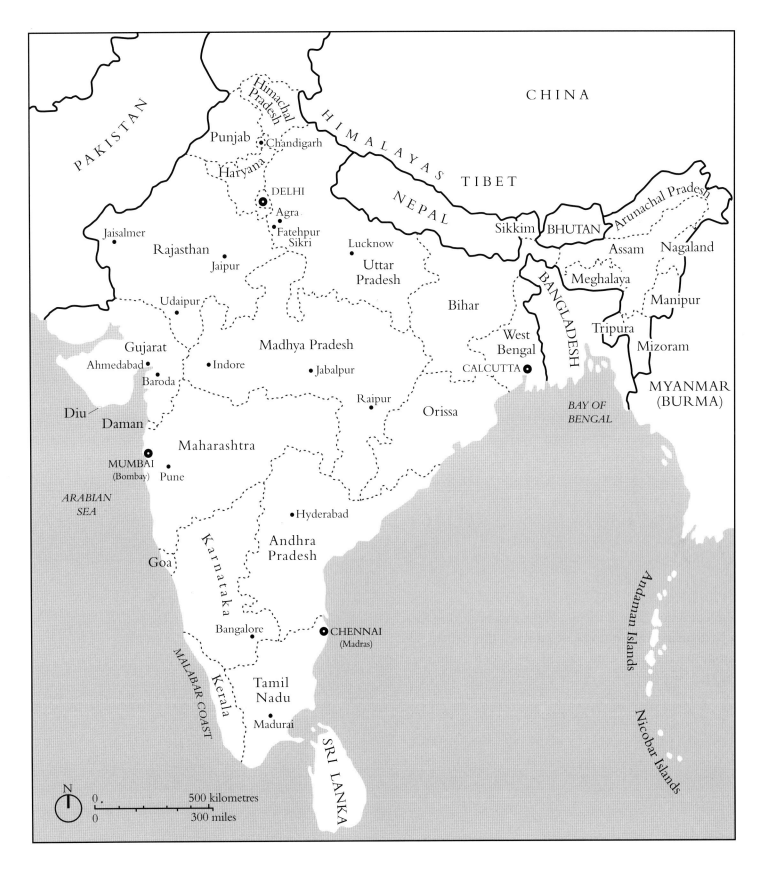

CHINA

PAKISTAN

Himachal
Pradesh

Punjab •Chandigarh

Haryana

H I M A L A Y A S    T I B E T

N E P A L

DELHI

Agra
Fatehpur
Sikri

Jaisalmer

Rajasthan

Jaipur

Lucknow

Uttar
Pradesh

Sikkim   BHUTAN   Arunachal Pradesh

Assam   Nagaland

Meghalaya

Manipur

Udaipur

Gujarat

Ahmedabad

Baroda

Diu

Daman

Madhya Pradesh

Indore

Jabalpur

Bihar

West
Bengal

BANGLADESH

Tripura

Mizoram

MYANMAR
(BURMA)

CALCUTTA

Raipur

Orissa

BAY OF
BENGAL

Maharashtra

MUMBAI
(Bombay)   Pune

ARABIAN
SEA

Hyderabad

Andhra
Pradesh

Goa

Karnataka

MALABAR COAST

Bangalore

CHENNAI
(Madras)

Kerala

Tamil
Nadu

Madurai

SRI LANKA

Andaman Islands

Nicobar Islands

N

0          500 kilometres

0          300 miles

the past has surprised so many of Doshi's followers, also raises the issue of expressionism, or what Colin St John Wilson has called 'the hidden agenda of modernism', and resuscitates the earlier modernist debate about mechanization versus craft. Today India shares perhaps only with Morocco the combination of craft skills and decorative traditions that allows the exploration of integrating ornament and structure. The mosaic of broken china pieces covering the Gufa shells is a reminder of the possibilities that such exploration still holds.

Doshi's work is a compelling mixture of the modern and the traditional, containing the most fundamental aspects of each, without being deflected by superficial forms. For those who feel that the most significant cycle of Modernism has just begun, as well as for those attempting to interpret tradition in a meaningful way, Balkrishna Doshi presents a consistent approach.

That consistency is manifest through his ability to structure synthesis rather than hoping it will happen by accident, with equal parts of the equation from East and West, if those designations still have any meaning in a world in which the distance from an epicentre at Greenwich is increasingly meaningless. Doshi's own culture is so rich and venerable that it is extremely difficult to isolate individual points as being of relative importance in his mental source book, but there are

consistent clues. Having settled in Ahmedabad in 1955, Doshi has assimilated regional Gujarati culture. His office in Ahmedabad has compiled a list of 'must see' buildings with locations indicated on a map to help interested visitors navigate around the city. The implication behind the list is that these are the sites in the city that Doshi admires most and that seeing them will assist in understanding his work.

Located at the western crux of the continent, Gujarat is a mushroom-shaped region with an extensive coastline on the Arabian Sea and two deep, fjord-like gulfs that cut into it at the northwest and southeast. Its strategic location, for maritime trade to Iraq, Iran, the Arabian Peninsula, east African coastal cities such as Zanzibar and Lamu, and to Asian countries such as Burma, and for inland trade to northern India, has historically assured prosperity in the region and it is no coincidence that Gujaratis have a reputation as pragmatic and cosmopolitan businessmen. They are fiercely loyal to their region and yet worldly: the necessity to survive through trade has given them a uniquely double view.

Doshi has personally conducted extensive research into the various residential typologies in Gujarat in a variety of mercantile communities, such as the Bohras.[1] He has traced this group from the port city of Khambat to more than a dozen other cities in Gujarat, as their

Traditional Gujarati buildings employ intricately carved stone brackets to support deep overhanging eaves for shade, often around a rectangular central courtyard.

numbers and prosperity increased, identifying their own neighbourhoods, or Bohravads, in each case. Significantly, he has found that these have either developed organically or have been laid out in a gridiron pattern which Doshi attributes to their exposure to Western influence. Their wealth has also allowed the Bohras to use elaborate ornament on their houses, which in some cases copies the decor of the British with whom they traded.[2]

Doshi's interest in the evolution of vernacular residential typologies has not been confined to the Bohravads, however, but extends to other old residential precincts, or *pols*, in Ahmedabad. Located inside the medieval circuit of the city, more than 350 of these socially identifiable units are typified by densely packed clusters of row houses. These are of the Gujarati type, with a large central court beneath a covered skylight, surrounded by balconies leading to the bedrooms above, a living/reception area on axis with the front door beyond the court, and with a swing-seat suspended by chains as a prominent piece of furniture in this room. The ornamentation on the facades of the traditional Gujarati houses in the *pols* of Ahmedabad is not duplicated on the interior. The external ornamentation, characterized by *jharokas* or projecting balconies, intricately carved facades and brackets, acts like an extended *mashrabiya*, the carved latticework wooden window typically found on vernacular houses throughout the Middle East, providing privacy from the outside world. The interior of the Gujarati house, on the other hand, is far more visually accessible to visitors.

The Vastu-Shilpa Foundation for Studies and Research in Environmental Design, established by Doshi to research the vernacular residential architecture of the region, is currently surveying the entire medieval area of Ahmedabad, and each of the *pols* in turn, not only to provide a resource for the office in their urban-planning commissions, but as a public service and invaluable historical document as well. This effort is intended to inform the design process and is clearly traceable in it. Yet Doshi is not an exceptional case as an architect singlemindedly attempting a synthesis between two cultures. His individual architectural agenda is symptomatic of the same kind of foreign and local synthesis that cosmopolitan Gujaratis themselves have been practising for centuries. He describes the predicament of 'having to look back at traditions almost hypnotized by the past and without any clear view of the present or hint about the future'. He considers his focus on the past to be an attempt to examine what is tangible and close to him: that is, the rich collection of historical monuments that are at the same time real, comfortable and predictable.

Le Corbusier, Mill Owners' Association Building, Ahmedabad 1954.
Bridges and ramps lend the rectilinear structure a powerful dynamic quality.
Balconies and shaded courtyards, as in traditional Gujarati architecture,
offer protection against the sun. Concrete, however, has not fared well
in the harsh climate.

# INTRODUCTION

Louis Kahn, Indian Institute of Management, Ahmedabad 1962–74.
'When one walks around the complex silently,' wrote Doshi in 1975,
'either in cool winter or in hot and stark summer, one gets the vibrations
of conversations, dialogues, meetings and activities. The spaces that are created
for these activities link the entire complex.' Kahn used local brick for economy,
but it also serves to reflect the immediate environment. Arches refer back to
older architectural traditions.

**Below left and opposite below** 'The court is a meeting place of the mind,
as well as the physical meeting place.' Freestanding lecture halls and faculty
offices face each other across a wide central courtyard, linked by shady
walkways, with a library and dining hall at either end.

**Right and opposite above** Dormitories are integrated rather than separated
from the main buildings. Kahn promoted the feeling of a monastery, allowing
both privacy and interaction.

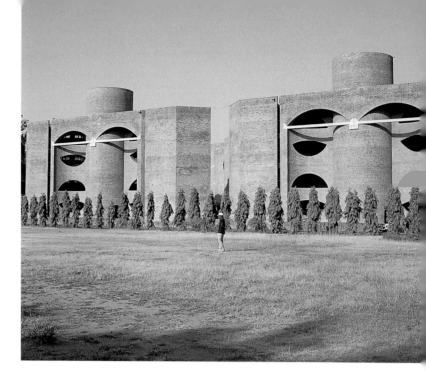

Buildings by Le Corbusier and Kahn constitute the modern Western component of these monuments on the Vastu-Shilpa list of places of architectural interest in Ahmedabad. They include the Sarabhai and Shodan houses, the Sanskar Kendra museum and the Mill Owner's Association Building (all by Le Corbusier) and the Indian Institute of Management (by Kahn). The rich coexistence of modern milestones in Ahmedabad, which were both influenced by Doshi and have been a continual source of theoretical nourishment for him, is an overwhelming reminder of the diversity and singular magnitude of his background. No other living architect

in India has had the breadth of experience he has had, and yet Doshi views that experience as both a blessing and a curse: 'even though I learned from great masters, I was nevertheless educated outside myself. This is why I have tried to become a son of the soil, to go back and see what it's really like to cast off the skin as a snake would and *become* again.'[3]

Sources that are less recognizable to the Western eye, such as the mosque and tomb complex of Sarkhej, the Jami Mosque of Ahmedabad, the Masjid-e-Nagira in the town centre, the Hatheesingh Jain Temple opposite the Darwaja, and the Adalaj and Dada Hari step wells, have a particularly strong resonance for him as important resources in his own region. Built as a mosque and tomb complex in 1457 for Ahmedshah Khattu and Queen Raja, the Sarkhej group is spatially intricate, with a vast interior courtyard and rectangular artificial lake, which served as a summer pavilion for the king and queen and which is also the burial place of a revered Muslim saint, spiritual guide to Sultan Ahmed I. In spite of its remote location, eight kilometres from Ahmedabad, Sarkhej is filled with people all day long who treat it as a communal meeting place and home away from home. It is especially popular at sunset when families and young lovers go there to enjoy the cool of the evening. Obviously the same cannot be said for Le Corbusier's Mill Owner's

**Above**  Jain temple tower, Ahmedabad.

**Left and opposite**  The mosque and tomb complex of Sarkhej (1457), near Ahmedabad. Built next to an artificial rectangular lake, the central courtyard is a popular meeting place.

**Above and opposite** Jami Masjid (Friday Mosque), Ahmedabad (1424). The complex of interlinked courtyards, arcades and walkways feels like a complete self-sufficient entity, filled with people and activity.

Association Building (on which Doshi worked), which is usually virtually deserted at any time of day. The contrast in popularity cannot have been lost on Doshi in his considerations.

The Ahmed Shah, or Jami (Friday) Mosque complex of 1424, near the centre of Ahmedabad, has a vibrancy that is similar to Sarkhej, conveying the feeling that it is a city within a city, a self-sufficient entity in which one would be quite happy to live indefinitely. On any given day the Jami mosque is crowded with visitors, buying from the food and clothing vendors lining the axial avenue leading up to it; sitting at the open-air counters surrounding cooking stoves set up on the

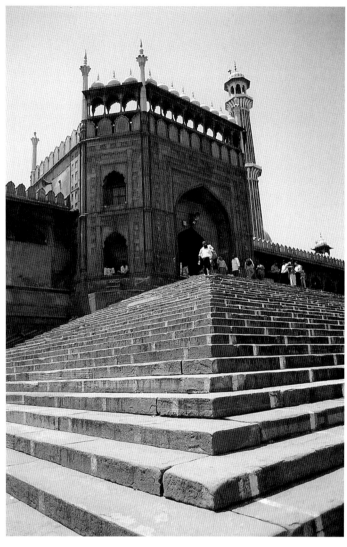

stairs and platforms adjoining them; or walking, sitting in groups, and sleeping inside the arcade surrounding the courtyard in front of the mosque, which is the coolest place to be in the complex, if not in the city itself. Some can be found in the mosque at prayer. This is the kind of activity and vitality which every architect dreams of encouraging in a design. If anything, the crush of people at the Friday Mosque can become oppressive.

There are constructive parallels that Doshi has transcribed, intentionally or subliminally, from these examples. The most obvious are structural clarity, hierarchy and amplification. The first two of these concepts were articles of faith for both Le Corbusier and Louis Kahn, enabling Le Corbusier to break the tyranny of the bearing wall (as in his 'five points') and as the almost mystical regard for the column and the notion of order described by Kahn. A structural overview of Doshi's work reveals that he uses the bearing wall to great effect principally because it makes more sense as a source of thermal mass in such a hot country. But in those instances in which piers or columns are integrated into the bearing-wall system, such as at the Indian Institute of Management at Bangalore (1977–85), the Gandhi Labour Institute in Ahmedabad (1980–84), the Madhya Pradesh Electricity Board in Jabalpur (1979–89), and the Bharat Diamond Bourse in Mumbai (1998), it demonstrates the extent to which this component has become a mediator between Modernism and tradition.

Structural amplification is a method by which a construction expands like a fugue in a vertical direction. In the remarkable historical example of the Adalaj step well, stairs are masterfully woven between the increasing rows of columns in descent to the water source. Doshi keeps on view at Sangath a beautiful bound survey of a stepped tank at Modhera, which is even more intricate than Adalaj, and such amplification is volumetrically legible in many of his projects, such as the Gujarat State Fertilizers Corporation in Baroda

**Left and above** Adalaj step well, near Ahmedabad 1502. The structure expands downwards towards the water source, with finely carved columns and staircases interlinked in a sort of descending fugue.

**Opposite** Madhya Pradesh Electricity Board (MPEB), Jabalpur 1979 (**above**); the walled city of Jaisalmer, Rajasthan (**below**). Doshi's MPEB resembles a city in miniature, integrated with the rocky, hilly environment.

(1964–69), the Electronics Corporation of India in Hyderabad (1968–71) and the Life Insurance Corporation in Ahmedabad (1973–76). In each of these there is not only a visible order, but the same kind of spatial refraction found at Adalaj, in which inner volume seems to expand exponentially.

Doshi has categorized eight principles in traditional architecture which he believes would greatly enrich contemporary practice. Moving beyond historical examples in his own region, he first cites the 'mythical sense' of space often evident in traditional architecture which is not simply confined to open or closed areas. Doshi attributes what he describes as 'the Hindu ability to transfer by ritual substitution', or to transform the function of a space by ritual use, as the reason for the cosmic dimension behind much of their architecture. Space can be 'modified according to the desire of the perceiver' and is never static.[4]

The kind of vibrancy found at Sarkhej and the Ahmedabad Jami Mosque is also characteristic of Hindu temples, and the transfer of energy that takes place between the walls, columns and spaces of the temple and the worshippers passing through them, either alone or in groups, has led Doshi to infer a second principle of 'transformation' between a building

**Left** Adalaj step well, near Ahmedabad 1502.

and the people that transcends functional use. More accurately described as a 'dialogue', this transfer underscores the important position that people occupy in Doshi's architecture, a surprisingly rare concept among those promoting various theories today. Heralded as a return to populism after the elitist excesses of the International Style, postmodernist approaches eventually deteriorated into a similar kind of insularity, as original intentions were forgotten. Robert Venturi, an early postmodernist, clearly blamed architects' fundamental tendency to distrust the public and preference for talking to each other through their work, as was made plain in both the later phase of modernism and theoretical reaction to it.[5] With the demise of the only formulated theory since the turn of the century that deliberately sought to embrace populism, the prospects for an architecture that would respond to people, rather than the nihilistic alternative of deconstructivism, became even bleaker. Deconstructivists proposed the deliberate antithesis of the human 'subject', who was 'decentred' by the interrogation of social institutions that it instigated, but this central agenda was not well understood by many practitioners and students, who copied the style just to be fashionable.

Oblivious to such superficial pressure, Doshi has persisted in his deep belief in the validity and

importance of 'human institutions', just as Louis Kahn did before him. This belief, which we may take as a third principle, is amplified by his own deep cultural experience and the popular evolution of new institutions. The 'dialogue' Doshi has experienced, which runs counter to the theoretical 'decentring' to which postmodern philosophers subscribe, also 'gives direction to the community at large', resulting in 'built forms which generate holistic experiences which finally become institutions'.[6] Much of Doshi's work is best understood as a continuation of this reaffirmation of belief in institutions, of recognizing, strengthening and creating them. It is no coincidence that many of his projects throughout his career have the word 'institute' in their title, such as the Institute of Indology,

the Indian Institute of Management and the Gandhi Labour Institute. His architecture assumes a collective will and, like a self-fulfilling prophecy, creates one through its physical presence.

The name of his office itself, the Vastu-Shilpa Foundation, is a ringing affirmation of Doshi's faith in the dialogue between people and architecture of which he speaks and the power of the dialogue to perpetuate old institutions and create new ones. The *vastu-shilpa* system is an oral tradition of passing down knowledge about building from generation to generation; it now co-exists with professional practice in the same way as *feng-shui* (spirit influences relating to one's living area) throughout Asia, although at a much more tectonic level. The design of a Hindu temple, for example, is

**Left, above and opposite** Fatehpur Sikri, near Agra, Uttar Pradesh. This Mughal complex consists of a series of linked courtyards and shaded rooms supported by carved pillars, within a walled enclosure.

always based on an ancient treatise called the *Shilpa-ratua*, which is metaphysical as well as scientific and mathematical. It also includes astronomy and magic. It allows for vernacular and regional variations because these have also been transmitted through an oral tradition that is easily adaptable.

A fourth, more specific principle is to follow a 'flexible rather than rigid approach to structure'. This is how a transformation of space from a mere static container to a place in which people actually feel a psychic interchange is best achieved. The Adalaj step well provides one example of this in the amplification of a trabeated structure, but Doshi refers more particularly to 'multiple, mixed structural systems', of the type found at the Madurai temple, or in the Mughal city of Fatehpur Sikri, which also ranks high on Doshi's list of favourite historical sources. Madurai, which is a series of complexes on slightly varying axes inside a walled enclosure, is a more compact example of the architect's idea of structure as a 'live instrument' that activates various layers of functional needs. In each of the multitude of enclosures and temples of various sizes crammed inside the Madurai circuit wall, space is modulated in a different way, from densely forested hypostyle hall to large rectangular inner court surrounded by a bearing-wall perimeter.

This notion of flexibility leads naturally to Doshi's fifth principle, of incorporating symbolism. He believes that such nuances can only be accommodated by a mixture of structural systems. Symbolically charged space must be designed as a receptacle for human activity, able to serve as a backdrop for each of the rituals, or important behaviour settings of life and take its essence from the incremental interactions that take place in it. There is a parallel here with Aldo Rossi's concept of a perpetuating permanence, or with a building such as the Basilica in Vicenza, which endures not because of stylistic hegemony, but because it has been able to accommodate a variety of uses over a long period of time in a dignified way.

To accommodate such nuances, as a sixth principle, Doshi also advocates amorphous, rather than finite forms used with multiple structured systems so that 'experience within them may be loose, meandering and multiple'. The massing that results from the mixture of trabeated and bearing-wall systems as described earlier at Madurai Temple, is one compelling model for such forms, as is the great temple at Tanjore, in which surfaces are 'dematerialized' by ornamentation. Doshi's awareness that such detailing was intentionally left incomplete as an expression of the futility of seeking perfection has shaped his attitude to design as an ongoing process that is never finished. Layering is another technique, in addition to ornamental detailing, that is frequently found in vernacular architecture to achieve the amorphous quality that Doshi describes; he has adopted it to great effect as a means of adding richness to even the lowest-budget project, such as the Life Insurance Corporation Project in Ahmedabad or the Aranya Low-Cost Housing Project at Indore.

The structural and formal systems that he has adopted here have led Doshi to assimilate a seventh principle of the *Vastu-Purusha Mandala* to ensure minimum standards of health and hygiene in each project. *Vastu* (environment), *purusha* (energy) and *mandala* (astrology) are combined in a diagram that has evolved to assist builders in determining proper orientation. North relates to the Lord of Wealth, south to the Lord of Death, east to the Lord of Light (the rising sun) and west to the Lord of the Wind. The centre is attributed to the Lord of the Cosmos. Following this chart has generally indicated a southwest orientation, favouring the prevailing breeze and also has defined the use of a central courtyard.

As an eighth and final principle, Doshi seeks timelessness in his architecture much as Louis Kahn did when describing this quality in historical precedents as 'open-endedness'. Foresight has allowed his work to withstand changes. His earliest projects have withstood use well, allowing them to remain as durable examples for a new generation of Indian architects, who look to him as an example.

# 1
# Institute of Indology, *Ahmedabad, 1957–62*

Indicative of Doshi's early affinity for Corbusian devices, such as a strict module, reinforced concrete frame and screen and protective overhanging roof, the Institute of Indology is also an object lesson in his ability to synthesize these with vernacular elements. The Institute is located on a lush 3.7-hectare site donated by the Ahmedabad Education Society on the periphery of Gujarat University. It houses a collection of ancient manuscripts which had previously been stored below ground in Jain temples. A sudden change to an air-conditioned environment would have been destructive, paradoxically, since they required similar conditions of temperature and humidity to remain intact. Doshi responded with a linear building that stretches across the site to present a long facade to the prevailing breeze. The building is partially recessed into the ground so that the manuscripts are stored in a half-basement cooled by cross-ventilation, which enters and leaves the lower level through distinctive angled air scoops. This creates an entry level which is a half storey above grade, reached by a raised bridge that connects the entrance deck with the street.

The Institute of Indology was built initially to house a valuable collection of ancient documents. Having been stored below ground in a Jain temple (**right**), the collection had to be preserved in similar conditions, without air-conditioning, using natural cross-ventilation.

**Top, above, right** Jantar Mantar, Delhi. The geometric forms create striking silhouettes, echoed by Le Corbusier's Parliament building in Chandigarh.

**Above right and opposite** Le Corbusier, Parliament building, Chandigarh 1962.

It was originally intended that there would be moat-like pools between the building and the street. These have since been replaced with a lush magical garden with hibiscus, bougainvillaea and peacocks. William Curtis mentions the architect's reference to the raised plinth of a Jain *apashraya* in Ahmedabad, which also has a balcony sheltered from the sun by an overhanging roof.[7] The key idea here is the marriage of this Jain typology and an effective vernacular technique of earth berming and cross-ventilation with the Modernist prototype introduced into India by Le Corbusier in the Palace of Justice of Chandigarh and the Mill Owner's Palace and Villa Shodan in Ahmedabad.

The second museum phase of the Institute was added at the southern edge of the site, behind the existing building and separated from it by a paved courtyard. This courtyard accelerates the process of convective cooling, originally established by the system of opposing air vents. The garden was chosen instead of the planned pools between the building and the street, to promote the convective effect. Cool air is retained by the surface area of plants and grass in the garden, especially in the evening, and in the morning, as the sun begins to heat the paved courtyard, the rising hot air that is generated begins a convective cycle, drawing the cooler air from the garden through the subterranean manuscript vaults and the open

Left  The heat generated by the hard-paved courtyard behind the Institute causes hot air to rise, creating a convective cycle which draws cooler air from the garden (**below left**) through the building. The breeze flows through wide doors hinged at a mid-point (**below right**). Traditional Gujarati features are incorporated within the strict contemporary order: balconies, rows of pillars such as those found in Gujarati mosques and palaces, and deep overhanging eaves to provide shelter from the sun.

middle atrium. The atrium is entered through Doshi's characteristic wide-leaf doors. The doors, hinged at the third point rather than at the corner, are really more akin to a wall that may be opened to allow in as much air as possible. Similar doors are used at both the Secretariat and the main museum at Chandigarh by Le Corbusier, which are contemporary with the Indology project. The concrete shading screen in front of the southern facade of the building also recalls Le Corbusier's work.

As one of Doshi's earliest independent projects, the Institute of Indology demonstrates the initial rationalization of the International Style to conform more precisely to the Indian context in environmental, historical and technical aspects. Le Corbusier's cursory appropriation of a studied selection of national symbols, however sensitively and perceptively chosen and applied, were only token gestures at a certain level. Such metaphors as the funnel of the Assembly Building at Chandigarh with its echoes of the Jantar Mantar Observatory in Delhi, or crescent roofs directly

The lush garden replaces the moat-like pools that were initially intended to divide the building from the street. The cool air is drawn through the basement of the building where ancient manuscripts are housed and out to the hotter paved court behind.

compared to turbans and bulls' horns in his sketchbooks, remain abstract references with little relevance to the reality of the lives of the citizens of the new city. They do not offset, for example, the cultural myopia evident in the act of specifying concrete on a project of such monumental scale in a country that was not equipped either to import it or to erect the scaffolding and use the pneumatic hoses required to place it, or of designing an automobile-based capital for a bicycle economy. Women and children filled reed baskets with concrete that were then carried on their heads up bamboo scaffolding to the top of the multi-storey formwork necessary to make such grand statements. These considerations were not lost on Louis Kahn, who was as much a mentor as a friend to Doshi. Although he did not find an alternative to concrete at Dacca, he at least indicated that he recognized local exigencies and technical shortcomings by designing the elevations to express and accommodate the various stages of bamboo scaffolding and manual placement.

Residents of Chandigarh, however, today proudly defend their city. These issues are never one-sided. Le Corbusier did manage, with Doshi's insistence, to make the city the final embodiment of Ebenezer Howard's Garden City ideal, with broad green avenues and covered planted arcades being the most memorable

legacies of that utopian concept. The Institute of Indology is a reminder of the complexity of attempting to judge Modernist interventions in India and elsewhere at the time it was built. Doshi has extrapolated the best of the Chandigarh lexicon and made it more humane and realistic, the twin traits of his Gujarati heritage. While the material is the same, the scale of the concrete screens on the southern elevation is much more modest; his willingness to break the structural module to allow for the necessity of an expansion joint reveal the mixture of idealistic and pragmatic elements that continue to make his architecture a paradigm for younger Indian architects, as well as for foreign practitioners sensitive enough to seek guidance before they make an intervention in the region.

Doshi has always sought to learn from the past rather than simply to repeat it. Concrete is not well suited to the hot humid climate of Gujarat, no matter what precautions are taken, and both the Institute and the Ahmedabad School of Architecture that followed in 1966–68 have suffered externally since they were built, leading him to search for new solutions.

Institute of Indology, second phase. Doshi employed a concrete frame in the Modern tradition, but the material has visibly suffered from the ravages of the extreme climate.

# 2
# School of Architecture, *Ahmedabad, 1968*

The Centre for Environmental Planning and Technology (CEPT) was sponsored by the Ahmedabad Education Society (AES), a premier voluntary non-profit organization established in 1935 devoted to the cause of education at all levels in several branches of learning. The School of Architecture was started in 1962, offering an undergraduate programme in architecture. This was followed by a postgraduate programme in planning under the School of Planning in 1972. In 1982, the School of Building Science and Technology was established. The School of Interior Design was founded in 1992.

Since 1994, CEPT has been registered as a separate Society and a Public Trust. CEPT is an autonomous institution offering education in the multi-disciplinary fields of the built environment, with its own diplomas for various academic programmes, which are recognized by the government. It is managed by the Governing Council, consisting of nominees of its parent body AES, government experts from the professions and industry, as well as its faculty.

'An open place with hardly any doors': Doshi's dictum for the School of Architecture expresses the sense of freedom he seeks in his design.

**Left** Angled windows let more light into double-height drawing studios, giving a feeling of airiness and space; shaded meeting areas promote free social interaction. The recesses created by the concrete frame (**below right**) give shade to the side of the building and to the rooms within.

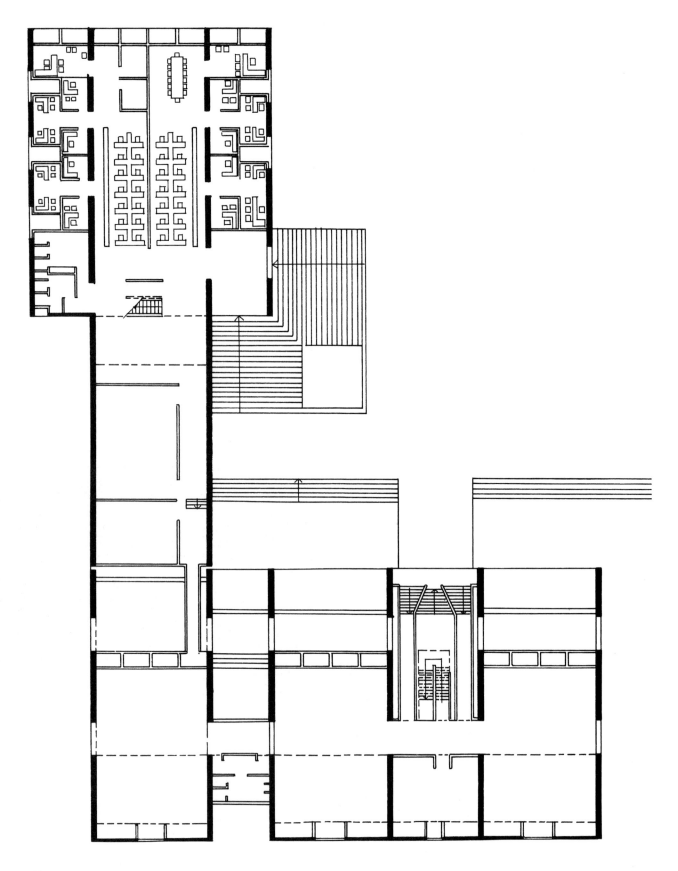

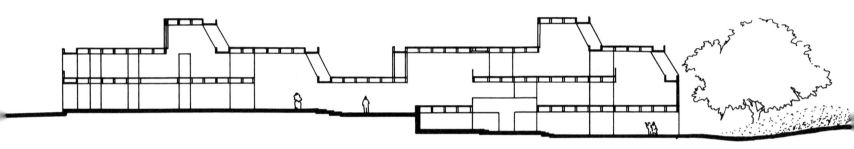

CEPT has a 5-acre campus near Gujarat University, accommodating the Vikaram Sarabhai Community Science Centre, the Hatheesingh Visual Arts Centre, the Husain-Doshi Gufa and the Kanoria Centre for Arts.

Doshi's primary concept for the School of Architecture was that it should be 'an open place with hardly any doors', and he was determined to use such accessibility not only as a metaphor for academic freedom, but also for environmental responsiveness. To do so, he used an L-shaped configuration based on parallel bearing walls on a north–south axis to capture and direct prevailing breezes through the studios, offices and classrooms. Working with the hilly contours of a site that was occupied by brick kilns when it was purchased by CEPT, Doshi decided to treat both inside and outside as educational space, refining Le Corbusier's notion of the open area under buildings raised on *piloti* to become shaded, naturally ventilated gathering areas.

**Opposite**  The long side of the L-shaped plan is exposed to the prevailing wind. A funnel-shaped entrance under the south facade (see photograph, **above**) is designed to direct the breeze through the building.

**Top**  Side elevation. The school is recessed into the landscape.

**Top** A hard courtyard draws cooler air up from the garden by convection.

**Above** Doshi: 'the space underneath is active and multi-functional, designed for sun protection and exposure to the breeze.'

**Right** Recesses protect from the sun; angled windows let in maximum light.

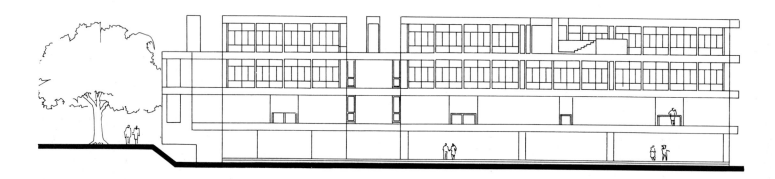

**Above** North elevation.

**Right** Covered 'streets', shaded passages and outdoor rooms allow 'free scope to teach and learn anywhere' (Doshi). These sheltered porticoes and promenades evoke an ancient Greek stoa.

The sensitive understanding of convection demonstrated at the Institute of Indology, completed just before the School of Architecture, prompted the architect to drop the studio complex one entire level and face it toward a grassy knoll and heavily planted part of the site. This complex presents the shortest, solid elevations to the hottest east–west axis. The longer classroom wing extends to the south and delineates one edge of a harder-surfaced plaza on the opposite side of the studio wing, which draws cool air contained in the green area through the open, shaded rooms below.

While this partially submerged outdoor room is a favourite meeting place for students, the entire school is extremely accessible and user-friendly and always hums with activity. The studios are high and airy, with north light from angled glass monitors, and wide doors which serve more as panels hinged at the third point, giving unhindered visual access to the outside and allowing a free flow of air. The first impression a visitor has of the School is of this permeability; this extends to Doshi's familiar outdoor covered 'streets' that are an effective way of joining disparate pieces together in many of his projects. They take on heightened significance here as representations of the *stoa* (or shaded promenade) used by peripatetic philosophers in ancient Greece and are especially welcome in the even hotter environment of Gujarat. This Western equivalent, however, with all of its obvious relevance to the university is layered over

**This page and opposite** Artists' studios near the School of Architecture. Outdoor rooms in the cooler air of the gardens allow work to continue in extreme weather conditions.

obvious recollections of shaded village streets like those in Jaisalmer, where *jharokas* (balconies) project out over narrow lanes and open balconies allow cool breezes to flow through unhindered.

The artists' studios, near the School of Architecture, are even more permeable. Their logical balance between an interior studio and exterior equivalent covered by a concrete frame roof reveals Doshi's pragmatism, and reflects a similar range of sources. The Western component here is more contemporary. The parasols and concrete 'egg crates' used as a shading device on the Mill Owner's house and the Villa Shodan have been adapted as covered outdoor platforms to be used for sculpture and crafts during times of the year when working indoors would be oppressive. There is

less brick used on the studios and so they have not suffered as much from the hot, humid climate.

The Husain-Doshi Gufa (see pp. 130–55), which is also near the school, shows the extent of the lessons learned about material performance in the thirty-five years since CEPT was built. The white ceramic mosaic that covers the shells, which can be hosed and scrubbed to ward off the omnipresent green fungus, is the result of a long process of trial and error that began at the school. Its brick surfaces have not fared well over time, but this superficial condition does not substantially detract from the achievement that the School of Architecture represents. It remains the premier professional institution in India, with a growing international reputation for excellence.

# 3

# Gujarat State Fertilizers Corporation, *Baroda, 1964–69*

Doshi's deliberate focus on institutions and his active involvement in Louis Kahn's Indian Institute of Management (IIM) at Ahmedabad in the mid-1960s has resulted in a slowly evolving theoretical position on the intrinsic character of such a large complex. He has been fortunate in having been able to secure the commissions to do so, which have allowed him progressively to put these ideas into practice. Following soon after Kahn's IIM, the Gujarat State Fertilizers Corporation (GSFC) in Baroda, completed between 1964 and 1969, marks the beginning of this evolution and there are many similarities between it and its immediate predecessor. Such vast complexes are the result of Nehru's determination to close the gap quickly between Third World states and developed nations as soon as possible after Independence, to catapult the nation into the industrialized world. As such, management institutes have been key instruments in this rapid change, homes away from home for the future bureaucratic elite of the country and those that teach them, with all of the attributes of a small self-contained township. GSFC is technically a corporate training facility, but still conforms to the type, a township of 1800 dwelling units designed to reflect the hierarchical status of the inhabitants.

From the beginning of his career, Doshi has been

**Above and opposite** Thick brick walls and brick paving in combination with traditional Gujarati features – courtyards, terraces and balconies – provide insulation and shade from the harsh sun.

determined to break the monotony so commonly found in new housing projects in India and to reflect socio-cultural patterns, climate and aesthetics, regardless of the economic status of the inhabitants. Doshi has described the restrictions he has had to face:

In large township projects where the government controls finances, there is a definite pattern of rules and conditions to be followed in spite of locational needs or changes in basic costs of materials. The projects usually emphasize the size and area of rooms, rather than living concepts: the four-wall room instead of a place, the living shell instead of a house. As a result, housing in India has always remained a package of boxes and not housing. There is very little attempt to elevate the standard of the overall living environment owing to the wrong emphasis on the notion of a formal living pattern. In my projects, I have tried to work the other way around; to create the pattern of old communities which are still valid and cherished by the inhabitants in an area, a pattern still seen even today in the old cities of India, such as Ahmedabad, Jaipur, Udaipur, and Jaisalmer. The elements which traditionally have converted adverse climatic conditions into comfort are again used, such as verandahs, courts and narrow streets. These solutions are born out of direct needs and their informal character is the reason for their survival.[8]

A pattern of roads around the township provides access, while ensuring the central zone remains free of motor traffic. The roads, which are planted with trees for shade, are oriented to reduce the adverse effects of the sun.

These elements are clearly some of the principal components of GSFC, based on thick brick walls and brick paved streets and pedestrian ways, court-yards, balconies and terraces. The result is an overall impression of substance and shade, protection from the harshness of the elements inside a durable, sympathetic world that the architect has provided. Cantilevered landings at the end of generous sculptural stairways, inside courts and bridges from these landings that give access to upper levels, all contribute to the strategy of using every opportunity to provide shelter from the sun.

A central green, with an auditorium and a water tower as a vertical accent, is the focal point of the entire scheme, with all roads patterned on a diagonal axis, leading to it. A main, encircling ring road and cul-de-sacs at the end of each of the branches leading from it that serve all the housing, ensure that this central zone remains car-free. One of the clusters, on the southern edge of the ring road, is based on the repetition of a 25-metre-wide strip which alternately becomes a passage between the houses, the two houses joined at the side, and another passage. In this typology, in which the massive walls running parallel to the houses shield a courtyard as wide as the house itself, open space is

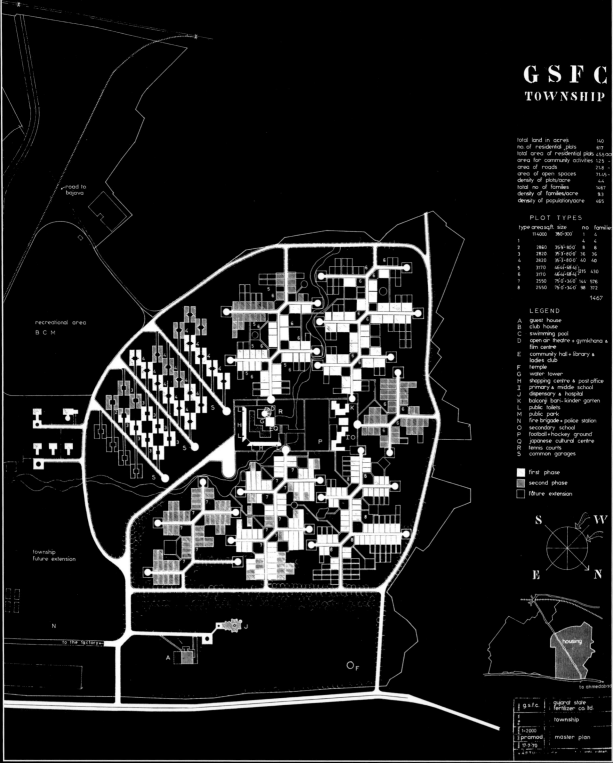

given prominence over the interior, which is mainly used for sleeping.

The straightforward, Kahnian geometry at Baroda, adjusted to accommodate courts, passages and squares so that they are more evenly distributed throughout the scheme rather than concentrated into the individual buildings themselves (as they are at Ahmedabad), is refined further in the Electronics Corporation of India at Hyderabad (built between 1968 and 1971), involving 2000 houses of eight different types, which were once again planned with standard dimensions to facilitate construction and lower costs. The encircling ring road is used once again as are zig-zag roads ending in cul-de-sacs that lead from it to serve housing clusters on both sides of a central 'cultural spine' that contains schools, a hospital, post office, police station, shopping and recreational facilities, and a vocational guidance centre to ensure employment in the community. Topography dictated a more linear arrangement of the spine and housing distribution on either side of it in this instance; but in the Aranya low-cost housing scheme at Indore of 1983–86 (which brought Doshi an Aga Khan Award for Architecture in the 1996 cycle), there is more freedom evident in the distribution of housing and services. Aranya displays a continuation of the ring road, zig-zag branch and central services model begun at Baroda, with a far more sophisticated,

less rigid intermixing of housing types and freedom in siting. This more closely approximates the conditions in a traditional community that Doshi has sought to replicate in a contemporary way.

The Indian Institute of Management at Bangalore is in many ways the culmination of this search, the logical bracket for Baroda twenty years earlier. Called 'a critique' of Kahn by Curtis, it is more accurately the realization of many goals, first among them to find a technique of expansion that allows cohesion as well as singular identity for each of the parts. A larger site allowed a variation of the ring-road frame at Bangalore: subsets of U-shaped access roads radiate from a central axial access spine, with clusters of housing grouped around each U. The main ladder-shaped complex has parts of all earlier schemes in it, but is far more intricate, perhaps due to a closer study of the Fatehpur Sikri model.

The story of GSFC in Baroda, then, is closely bound up with many projects of similar types and scope that followed, the start of a continuing process.

**Opposite** The site plan showing the ring road and diagonally arranged cul de sacs (upper left of the plan). The township is made up of clusters of different housing types. Clusters of house type 7 (lower left of the plan, and detail overleaf on p. 55) and type 8 (lower right of the plan, detail on p.57) are fitted together in a modular pattern.

**Below** Model showing housing clusters built around diagonal access roads. Courtyards are predominant features. The close network of short streets makes the township feel akin to a traditional village. Climatic and social considerations guided Doshi's design.

**Opposite** Site plan, plan and section, house type 7.

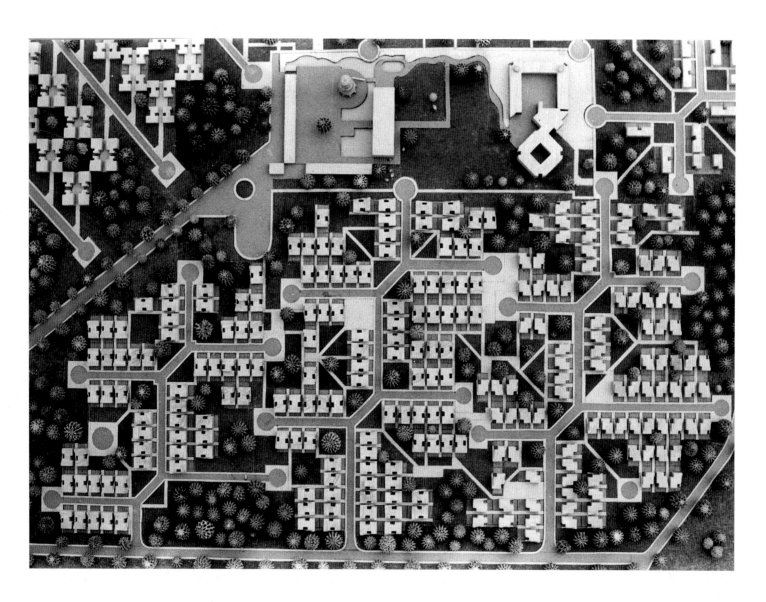

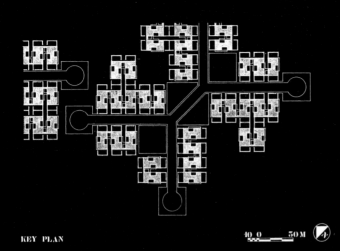

# GSFC
## HOUSE TYPE 7

1 STREET
2 PEDESTRIAN WALKWAY
3 ENTRY
4 COURT
5 LIVING
7 KITCHEN
8 BEDROOM
9 BATH
10 W. C.

KEY PLAN

10  0          50 M

PLANS

SECTION

10  0   2   4   6    8M

**Above** Narrow pedestrian walkways give the complex something of the atmosphere of an old, traditional pol (urban district). High walls built from local brick provide shade and privacy.

**Opposite** Site plan, plan and section, house type 8. Courtyards and pedestrian walkways are key features.

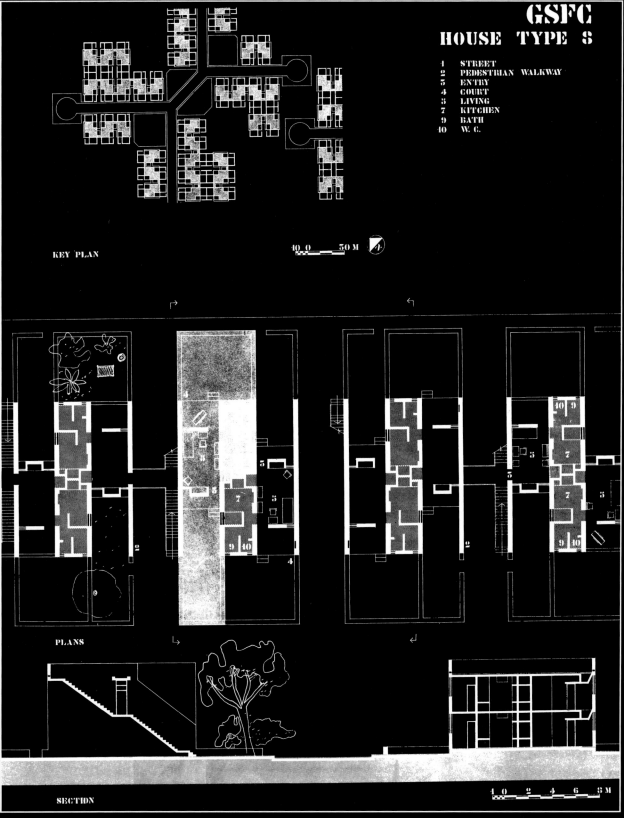

# GSFC
# HOUSE TYPE 8

1 STREET
2 PEDESTRIAN WALKWAY
3 ENTRY
4 COURT
5 LIVING
7 KITCHEN
9 BATH
10 W. C.

KEY PLAN

40 0     50 M

PLANS

SECTION

40 0 2 4 6 8 M

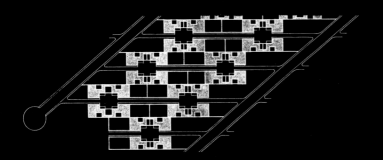

# GSFC
## HOUSE TYPE 2

2 PEDESTRIAN WALKWAY
3 ENTRY
4 COURT
5 LIVING
6 DINING
7 KITCHEN
8 BEDROOM
9 BATH
10 W. C.
11 STORE
12 TERRACE
13 SERVANT

KEY PLAN

40 0     50M

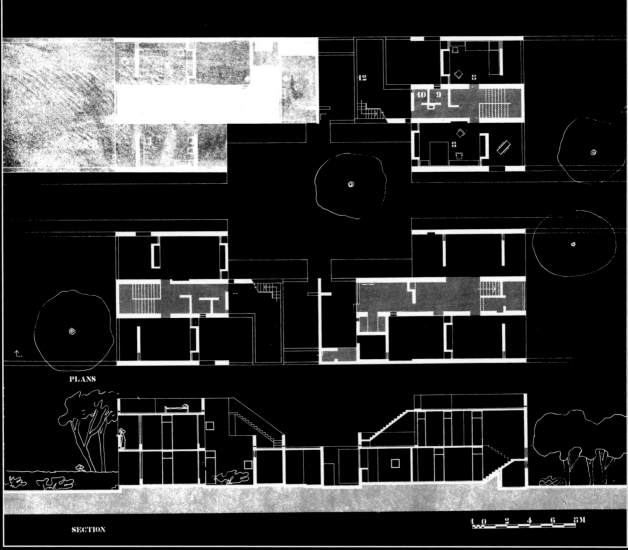

PLANS

SECTION

40 2 4 6 8M

**Above** Shaded verandahs overlook gardens. Local brick is both economical and provides practical insulation.

**Opposite** Site plan, plan and section, house type 2.

# 4

# Indian Institute of Management, *Bangalore, 1977–85*

T he Indian Institute of Management (IIM) at Bangalore is one of four institutes commissioned by the government shortly after Independence to train the future leaders of a new, industrialized society. The rise of a new middle class in India in the 1990s is partially a result of that decision.

Louis Kahn's Institute in Ahmedabad (1962–74) was based on an orthogonal system characteristic of his rational approach to planning. The heavy brick envelope of each of the units in that framework, pierced with huge circular and square openings, is placed in front of a second inner envelope as a means of layering that Kahn called 'wrapping ruins around the building', to create shaded glare-free spaces. Those spaces are inside each individual unit and the outdoor 'rooms' between them are mostly devoid of shade. Kahn relied upon this geometrical arrangement of units to bring order to a large and varied programme that includes classrooms, offices, a library and dining hall, dormitories and faculty residences, workers' housing and a market, all the components of a small self-sustaining village. Kahn employed the interlocking diagonal system that had been the inspiration of Ann Tyng in the design of the Bryn Mawr Dormitory in 1963. Kahn's layers provided terraces between the inner wall and outer brick envelope with arched openings widened by concrete relieving arches and this

**Above**  Louis Kahn, Indian Institute of Management, Ahmedabad 1962–74. The building is 'wrapped in ruins': Kahn built an envelope around a unit, and pierced it with wide openings to provide a ventilated insulating layer. Doshi adopted the technique for his Institute of Management at Bangalore (**opposite**).

intersticial space became a similar covered outdoor zone in blocks with other uses. The covered walkways between many of the blocks, while equally protective, fail to realize the vision Kahn had earlier described as 'a realm of spaces which may be connected by ways of walking and the walking is a protected kind of walking [which] you consider as high spaces together with low spaces and various spaces where people can sort of find the place where they can do what they want to do.'[9]

62

Louis Kahn, Indian Institute of Management, Ahmedabad 1962–74.
Huge round and square openings pierce the brick envelopes wrapped
around each building. Simple geometric forms are combined
harmoniously with brickwork and arches, familiar traditional
features. See also pp. 14–15.

Fatehpur Sikri, sixteenth century. Built by the emperor Akbar, the city was planned on Persian principles but constructed in the Indian manner. The buildings are linked by a series of courtyards – the progression of buildings is unified within a single walled enclosure. Shade is provided by fine stone screens, pavilions, walkways and balconies, beneath domed canopies and deep eaves supported by elaborately carved brackets, while air circulates freely.

**Above** Bhirbal Bhavan, residential apartments probably built to accommodate senior members of the Imperial harem.

**Opposite above** Diwan-i-Khas, the Hall of Private Audience.

**Opposite below** Khwabagah (House of Dreams), Akbar's sleeping chamber.

Balkrishna Doshi's IIM in Bangalore, which has been described as a 'critique' of Kahn's Ahmedabad Institute, deviates from some basic principles and fulfils others unrealized in the earlier project in significant ways. The main grouping of the campus, which contains administration offices, classrooms, laboratories and a library, is arranged as a datum in a ladder-like plan along a longitudinal axis, with student dormitories a short distance away, organized in interlocking squares at an angle to this axis. In the main campus plan, the 'outdoor rooms' are not as clearly defined as they are in the Ahmedabad essay; each of the open spaces is full of seemingly random pavilions to be used as teaching spaces, and there are walls that define terraces at various

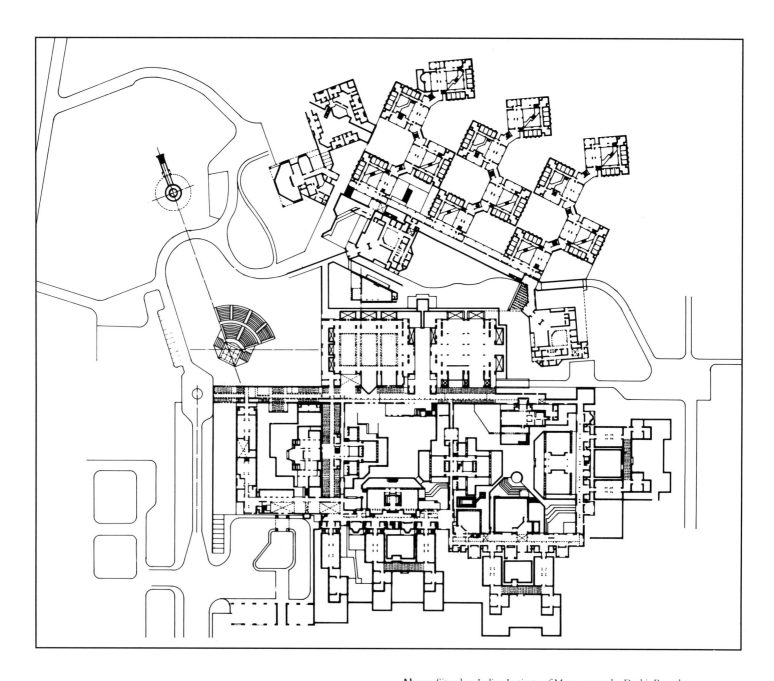

**Above** Site plan, Indian Institute of Management by Doshi, Bangalore. The forecourt and entrance are at the lower left of the plan. Dormitories are arranged diagonally around an interlocking series of courtyards, in the upper part of the plan. The main area – classrooms and faculty buildings – is a complex of courtyards linked by remarkable walkways or internal 'streets', some covered, some open to the sky, creating 'innumerable vistas or focal points for generating a dialogue with oneself' (Doshi).

**Opposite** Elevations. The Institute resembles a city in miniature, enclosed within a single unifying form.

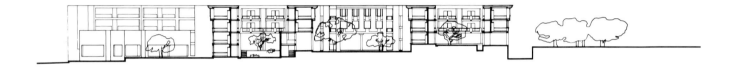

levels. What is most striking, however, are the corridors, more appropriately described as covered pedestrian streets, that join the diverse elements together. These were designed, according to Doshi,

> to provide innumerable vistas or focal points for generating a dialogue with oneself. These corridors are sometimes open, sometimes with pergolas and sometimes topped with a glazed skylight. To further heighten the spatial experience, the width of the corridors was modulated in many places to allow for casual eating and interaction to take place.

Soaring up to three storeys high in many places, these covered 'streets' literally activate the interstice that Kahn created at Ahmedabad, making it a continuous pedestrian thoroughfare, linking all of the various pieces of the plan and combining Kahn's terraces and walkways into one. With its dense population and tight family structure, India is a communal country and solitude is rare. By making it possible for students to have the chance to be alone if they want to be, Doshi offers a valuable alternative to the group encounters that are inevitable in this academic society.

The remarkable change that is evident from projects built only a few years earlier, such as the Electronics Corporation of India in Hyderabad (1971), indicates a conversion of sorts to a much more complex, historically based view. The Mughal city of Fatehpur Sikri, built by Emperor Akbar in the sixteenth century, was an obvious precedent for Doshi. One interesting

**Left** Windows shaded by concrete eaves.

**Opposite** Striated light effects make dramatic vistas. Corridors of columns beneath concrete pergolas create a rhythmic progression of light and shadow.

aspect of the choice of Fatehpur Sikri as a model is that on initial inspection the overall site plan seems to be based on a principle similar to the interlocking corners used by Kahn at Ahmedabad as a diagonal processional device, but on closer analysis the pattern is far more intricate and not nearly as regular. While some of the enclosures are symmetrical, they each contain elements that break strict axiality and they are joined to each other in dynamic, rather than static, proportional relationships. The pavilions placed inside the enclosures at Fatehpur Sikri gain in stature, rather than being diminished by their surrounding frames and they, in turn, prevent those frames from becoming repetitious. All of the principles now essential to his planning method, especially the use of multiple structural systems, mythical space, dialogue between architecture and people, symbolism, and amorphous form are present at Fatehpur Sikri and have been sensitively retranslated at Bangalore.

In a large complex such as IIM, the main problem facing the architect was how to make each portion distinct and yet to provide overall unity, to create institutional identity. The planning principles used in Fatehpur Sikri provided an example of such unity, as well as more subtle lessons about materials, consistency of details and hierarchy of scale, all evident at Bangalore.

INDIAN INSTITUTE OF MANAGEMENT

**Below** Staircase, showing Doshi's dramatic use of modern materials
to create an effect that is simultaneously monumental, airy and light.

**Opposite** Sections (**top and bottom**) and plan (**middle**) of pedestrian walkway.

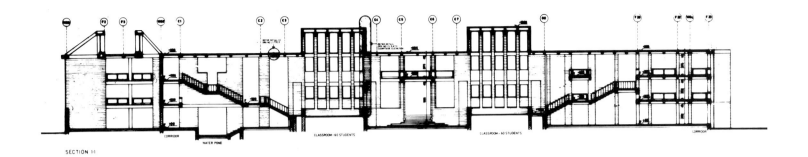

SECTION 1-1

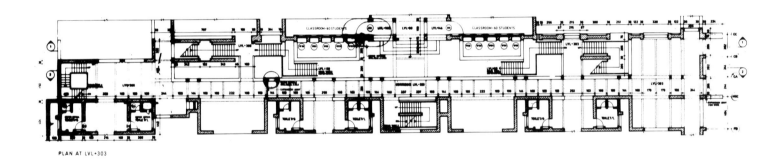

PLAN AT LVL+303

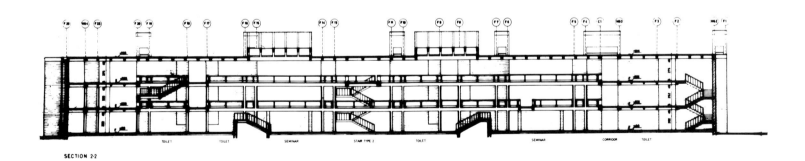

SECTION 2-2

# 5
# Madhya Pradesh Electricity Board, *Jabalpur, 1979–89*

At this point in India's industrial development, infrastructure is a critical concern. Newspapers and magazines constantly raise questions about the disparity between the nation's rising international market share and its lack of infrastructure. At its fiftieth anniversary of Independence, questions about the great disparities between rich and poor, the steadily growing, but still minority consumer class and the massive majority at subsistence level, seemed particularly relevant. In comparison with Communist China, which started on its solitary path of development at about the same time, some have even gone so far as to blame the freedom provided by democracy for India's secondary position in the development race, while others in its new management elite wonder aloud if the colonial legacy of bureaucracy isn't the culprit. There does seem to be a particular Indian penchant for creating procedures and then making them increasingly complex. This building for the Madhya Pradesh Electricity Board is an attempt to streamline that.

Electricity companies have historically been notable markers in national advancement toward industrialization, as witness the powerful tectonic diagrams of the constructivists, or the AEG building by Peter Behrens (1909–11). Behrens glorified the turbines he housed with an abstracted Greek temple, with references to a barn added to make recent rural

**Opposite and above** The Madhya Pradesh Electricity Board building is a large administrative centre comprising sixteen interlocking polygonal units distributed across a hilly, rocky site.

migrants feel more accustomed to the city and the world of industrial work. The response of Behrens's student Walter Gropius to his mentor's abstraction was to abstract history even further in the Fagus Shoe Last Factory (1911), a building which was particularly seminal in defining the International Style that soon followed.

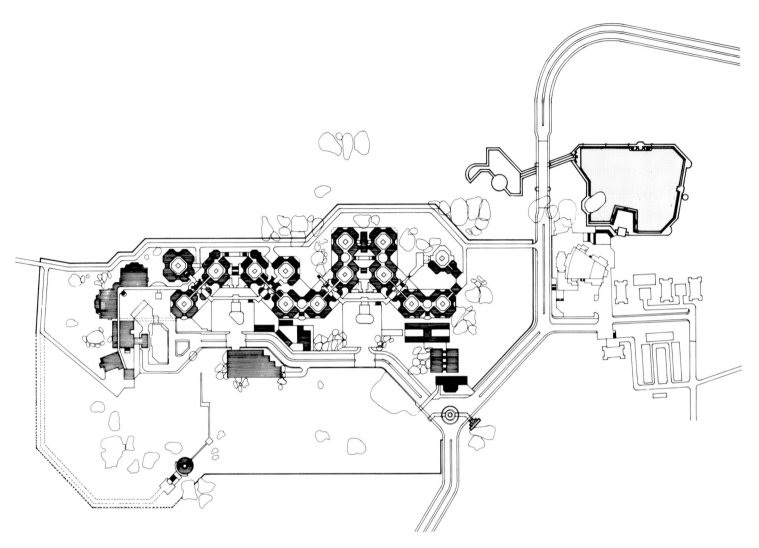

Perhaps appropriate to the central role that bureaucracy plays in Indian society, Doshi's iconic symbol of development at Jabalpur is an administrative centre, rather than a factory, and it has been designed to reflect the byzantine internal dynamics of such a system. Doshi has chosen an octagon as the basic building block of the complex, really a square with each corner clipped off, as another of his evolving strategies to accommodate a complex programme inside a unifying framework. This system, which has resulted in sixteen interlocking cells distributed across a hilly, rocky site along an east–west axis, might initially seem to be rigid, but works brilliantly as an organizing device for a large administrative complex on difficult terrain.

**Above** Site plan, showing interlocking components. The buildings are integrated with the rocky surroundings.

**Opposite above** The main entrance to the complex (shown on the left of the plan above).

**Opposite below** View of the building from the entrance portico.

**Following pages** Misting fountain, shaded walkways and courts.

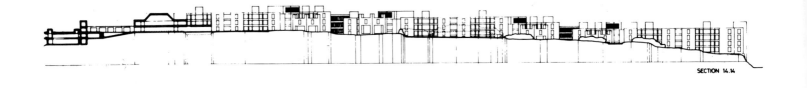

SECTION 14.14

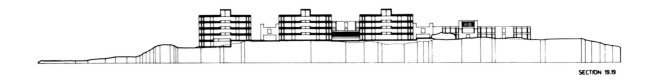

SECTION 19.19

SECTION 20.20

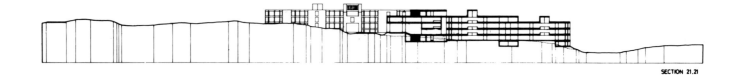

SECTION 21.21

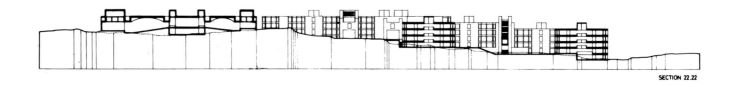

SECTION 22.22

SECTION 23.23

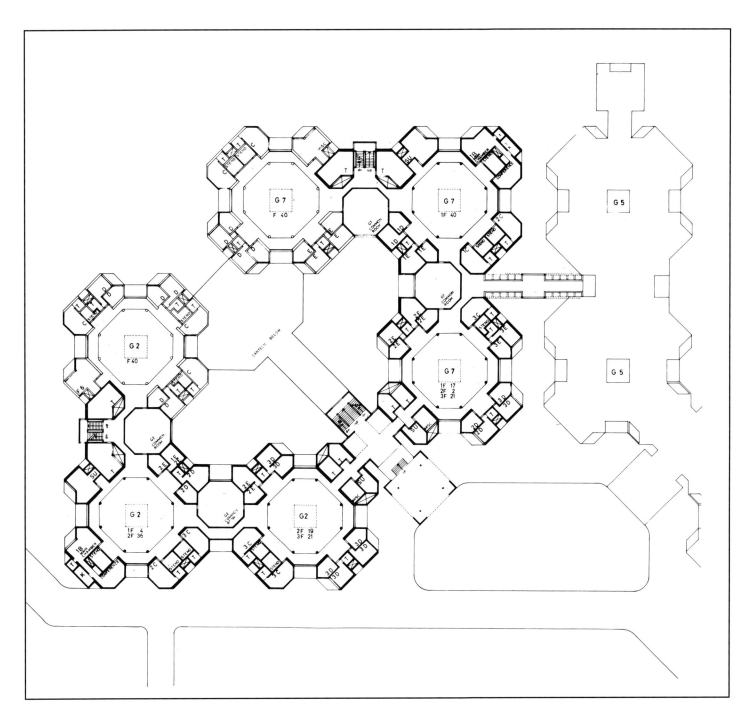

Sections and detail of plan. Sixteen interlocking cells are distributed across a hilly, rocky site. Doshi uses the octagon as a basic component of the complex, allowing flexible planning within a coherently organized framework. The varied angles of the structure also give more limited exposure to the sun.

**Above** The modular planning allows the building to be integrated into the hillside. Recessed openings, cutaways and overhangs provide shade.

**Opposite** Internal courtyard, showing balconies and shaded windows.

The deterministic plan, with service pods attached to the long sides of the clipped square, allows for vertical differentiation or stacking, and Doshi has used this to convey meaning. The office spaces, spread out across seven administrative departments and one main executive block, rise up as much as a sign of status as a way of accommodating function. Only the office areas have tall monitors which bring natural light down through central courts into work areas on various levels below. Other facilities, such as a recreational centre, 800-seat auditorium, dining room and kitchen, amphitheatre and shopping areas, as well as terraced gardens, bridges and shaded passages, have been located to vary the profile of the 43,500-square-metre 'city in

miniature' against the sky, keeping a building almost half a kilometre long from becoming monotonous.

The 'city in miniature' reference is not coincidental. This is a hill settlement reconfigured to conform to the post-industrial work ethic. Using Fredric Jameson's categories of the incremental growth of capitalism, it may be more accurate to say that the MPEB announces a point further along the curve from a post-industrial market economy, somewhere between the last two stages of monopoly and multinational integration.

In its crystalline geometry, clear definition of served and servant spaces and refined expression of the way light enters a wide variety of functions, as well as in its

abstract recollection of historical typologies, this project is one of the closest approximations to Kahn's rational language in Doshi's *oeuvre*. Other projects of similar scale, contemporary with the MPEB, such as the IIM at Bangalore, have been characterized as 'critiques' of Kahn, or as retakes by a local architect with a more thorough understanding of culture and environmental context. The MPEB project, however, is more of a reaffirmation than a critique. This is not Gropius turning his mentor inside out, but an instance of the unhesitating use of a system with full confidence in its logic. The most obvious Kahnian precedent is the Erdman Woman's Dormitory at Bryn Mawr College, credited to Ann Tyng, which has an equally clear distinction between served and servant spaces. A significant refinement at Jabalpur is Doshi's use of changes in the terrain to avoid internal stairs and elevators as a part of these servant spaces, which predominate at Bryn Mawr. The idea of continuous covered circulation used at Bangalore once again replaces Kahn's preference for more isolated solutions. Doshi's choice of local materials, such as strips of dark brown polished granite inset into the concrete frame and purple-brown stone chips in the plaster, echoes Kahn's use of purple slate panels inserted into a concrete frame at Bryn Mawr, the difference, once again, being contextural specificity.

**Above** Laid out over a long site, the level of the single building changes often, reflecting the contours of the hilly area. Angled steps echo the octagonal forms of the interconnected units.

**Opposite** View of Jabalpur. The MPEB project was designed as a city in miniature, reflecting the integration of social and industrial spheres.

# 6
## Sangath, *Ahmedabad, 1979–81*

The fame that Balkrishna Doshi enjoys in India is not universal, but Sangath is the best-known of all his work internationally. Sangath, which means 'moving together through participation' in Sanskrit, is a village-like enclave of distinct rectangular volumes aligned along a north–south axis inside a lush green compound on the outskirts of Ahmedabad. The participation it is intended to foster transcends the production of architecture and is described by the architect as 'the encouragement of activities in the fine and technological arts'. Doshi encourages fine-arts exhibitions and has provided space for craft workshops. The name of his firm, the Vastu-Shilpa Foundation, is Sanskrit for 'design of the environment'. This implies traditional construction and conveys a similar attitude of broad-based research, rather than a narrow focus on design alone, consistent with Doshi's general interest in Indian history, urbanism, arts and crafts.

While many architects use the opportunity of designing their own home as a chance to experiment with personal interests and new ideas, Doshi has extended that intention to his office as well. This cluster of rectangular units of various lengths is arranged in four parallel ranks, with a deliberate gap provided for an outdoor amphitheatre in their midst. Louis Kahn was fond of saying that the first school began when a person who did not realize he was a teacher began to

**Above** Amphitheatre, Sangath. In Sanskrit the word means 'moving together through participation'.

**Opposite** Glazed ceramic fragments set into the outer surfaces reflect heat and glare from the sun.

speak to people who didn't know they were students under a tree. The central court and amphitheatre at Sangath conveys that primal impression and is used for lectures and discussions under the green canopy that surrounds and shades it. Water running through a wide trough spills off the roof in a waterfall just behind the

SANGATH

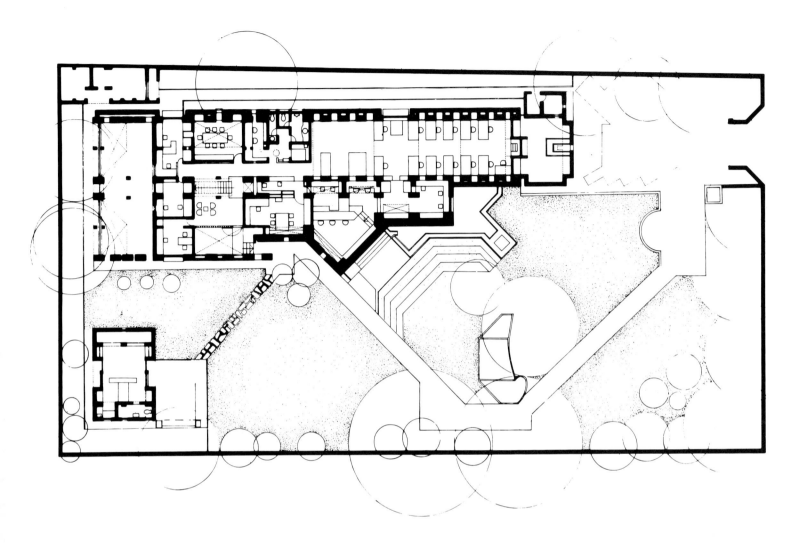

amphitheatre seating, contributing to the elemental framework completed by the material used to build the office. The first two ranks of rectilinear forms of Sangath on the west are dug into the earth as physical protection against the severe summer heat. The ranks rise up toward the east as the deck does, just at the angled mid-line created by the waterfall. The vaults, which are primary architectural features and impressions of the studio ensemble, are also made of sandwiched layers of ferrocement and ceramic 'fuses', or strands of clay, which were pressed together to become the formwork for a concrete shell applied by hand on top of it. In one of the first instances of a detail that has since become a centrepiece of Doshi's tectonic language, the waterproofed surface of the shells was

**Above** Site plan. Sangath represents Doshi's tour-de-force – principally the architect's office, it is also a centre for the exchange of ideas.

**Opposite** The amphitheatre court, with preliminary sketch. 'Schools began with a man under a tree, who did not know he was a teacher, discussing his realizations with a few others, who did not know they were students.' (Louis Kahn)

then covered with pieces of broken china. The hand labour and time required to do this are extensive and only conceivable and affordable in a country in which wage levels are very low and there is a well established history of meticulous detailed handicraft. Some analysts have constructed intricate references for the vaults: a positive manifestation of the negative vault found in the Maison Jaoul by Le Corbusier, the parity of vernacular village architecture in India, as well as the Greek

Vaulted roofs resemble those Doshi had seen in Egypt. They cover an interlinked network of rooms below ground; this affords protection from the heat, and presents a low profile.

**Opposite** Water cascades into a descending series of pools and channels. Light, shade, water and air – aspects of the natural elements – are celebrated in and around the building.

Islands, the apse of the Karli cave, transformed in elevation, the concrete vault of Kahn's Kimball Museum translated into earth. The reality is much more prosaic, as Doshi describes:

> the major design element, or roofing vault, owes its origin to a happy accident. Years ago, when designing a small, compact outhouse on the site, I asked a building contractor friend for roofing sheets. He only had curved corrugated sheets. Undaunted, I set about designing the outhouse and the results were visually striking. Much to my wonder, I found that the proportions of the vaulted roof in relationship to the base were similar to Indian temples and sought to re-create this proportion at a larger scale when designing Sangath.

Another possible precedent, albeit subconscious, is the Wissa Wassef Museum in Harraniya, Egypt, which Doshi had sketched while visiting the Aga Khan Award-winning project in late January 1978. The parallels that Harraniya presents are intriguing, since Wassef was once a partner of Egyptian architect Hassan Fathy, who deliberately set out to develop a singular architectural language for his country that would free it from foreign associations. Fathy and Wissa Wassef approached the problem from the Muslim and Coptic perspective respectively, but each arrived at a similar vault-and-dome language rendered in mud brick. They each felt that this represented the essence of Egypt's historical traditions and Fathy went so far as to claim that the combination of vault and dome had originated in the Middle East.

Wassef and Fathy sought meaning and authenticity in a clearly defined formal language that evoked, but did not literally copy, the past and used vernacular construction techniques to realize it. Formulating a recognizable image that appeared to be authentically Egyptian was to send the implied message that foreign styles and intervention were not welcome and that Egyptians were capable of deriving their own architectural language as they had done for millennia.

Doshi's nationalistic pride, independent spirit and desire for autonomy is certainly equally to, if not greater than, Fathy's, yet his method of expression has been different. His emphasis has not been on deriving a clearly recognizable 'Indian architecture', but on a logical, theoretical archaeology that will lead to the principles behind the form.

Sections and elevations. The low profile of the vaulted roofs conceals a network of interconnected spaces, extending below ground level. The varying roof heights inside, from single to double and triple-height rooms, are reminiscent of underground caves.

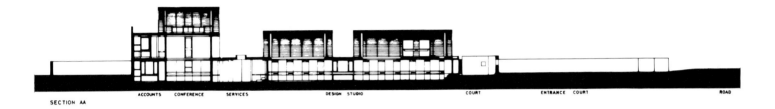

SECTION AA     ACCOUNTS    CONFERENCE    SERVICES      DESIGN STUDIO      COURT     ENTRANCE COURT       ROAD

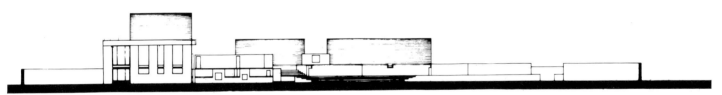

WEST ELEVATION

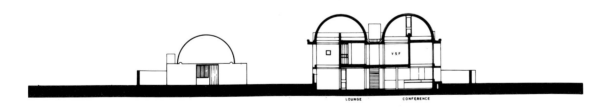

VSF

LOUNGE     CONFERENCE

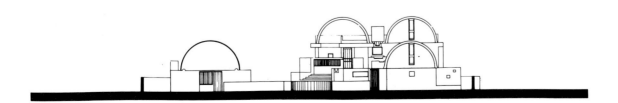

In shady gardens, terracotta pots link rustic materials and the built form. Traditional and modern forms are harmoniously combined.

**Above right and opposite** Water cascades from a fountain into a series of channels, which, like other outer surfaces, are covered with glazed china pieces.

The geometry of the Sangath's construction was defined by rules of the golden section and the Platonic circle. If the circle implied by the curve of the vaults was completed, the base would rest on the ground.

The arch and vault are venerable forms with emotive associations in both European and Asian history. In his great quest for timelessness, Louis Kahn selected the combination because of its substantial teleological descent from Roman through Romanesque construction. The Greeks rejected it for anything other than utilitarian use for the very reasons that it is so powerful at Sangath, believing the eye was led up from the ground back down to the ground instead of preserving the purity of the trabeated lintel that linked a temple to the horizon.

As an expression of Doshi's 'saturated thoughts on what architecture for a place should be' and 'attempt to build spaces suitable to the local climate and to develop structure and form which evokes a local ethos', Sangath is without parallel in his *oeuvre* and its impact transcends analysis. The golden section and square were used in determining the plan and section, the satisfying geometry of the Platonic circle, half-visible in the vault and implied in the height of the vault above the ground, is evident. The four elements of earth, air, fire and water are equally apparent, and yet Sangath touches a more elemental chord that goes beyond such rational considerations. It is the essence of architecture, regardless of cultural associations, and its strength defines Doshi best.

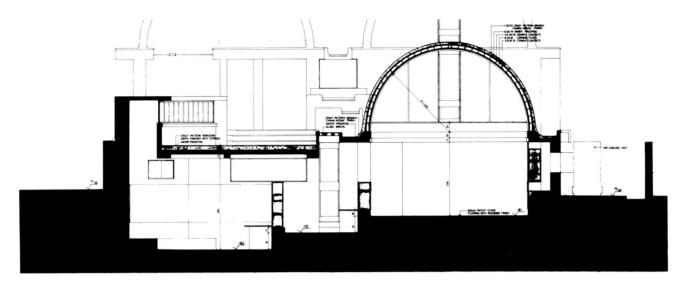

**Opposite and below** Traditional objects – terracotta pots, statues –
enhance traditional elements of the architecture. The whole building has
a satisfying proportion and balance, yet is also characterized by an uneven
rhythm and asymmetry that allies it naturally with its environment.

# 7

# Gandhi Labour Institute, *Ahmedabad, 1980–84*

Original sketches for this institute, perpetuating the ideals of one of the greatest leaders in contemporary Indian history, show a long, ledge-like plinth base with vaults emerging from it like huts on a stone plateau. That image captures Gandhi's great strength and dematerialistic humility, his realization of the enormous power that comes from simplicity and calm. Exigencies of irregular site boundaries and the formality expected of an institution altered that original vision, but the elemental sense of it has come through in the final design. Divided into offices for directors and assistant directors, a reception and exhibition space, boardroom, general staff offices, seminar rooms, a computer room, library, auditorium, dining hall, and a cluster of residences across from an outdoor amphitheatre at the back of the site, the institute is organized around a square central courtyard that gives the various spaces cohesion.

The entrance, which is hidden from the front gate and the court commonly used for arrival by car, is recessed with banks of stairs gradually leading up to it past a misting fountain used to defray the heat. The diagonal axis that Doshi has intentionally established from the gate to the front door generates a sense of mystery, as well as obliging visitors to see the front elevation in perspective, giving the impression of great dignity and strength. Penetration past the long walls of

**Above**  The approach to the Institute leads up a shallow series of steps past a misting fountain.

**Opposite**  The diagonal axis from the front gate to the front door allows the approaching visitor to gain a sense of the building's perspective. The lack of a monumental entrance means that the Institute feels accessible to all.

the director's office on the left and the auditorium on the right, when that axis changes from diagonal to orthogonal, heightens that impression and formalizes it. The high vertical scale and width of the first passage after entry, which is perpendicular to it and is

**Below** Looking south across the Institute, the importance of different open spaces can clearly be seen. Terraces, courts and an amphitheatre express Doshi's intention to use open spaces to 'tie the entire property together as an urban complex'.

**Opposite** Axonometric site plan. Doshi ingeniously combines an irregular site with regular square forms, and outside with inside space, achieving a harmonious sense of unity. The entrance is in the lower right-hand corner of the central courtyard, approached diagonally from the angled front gate via a progression of terraces, platforms and steps.

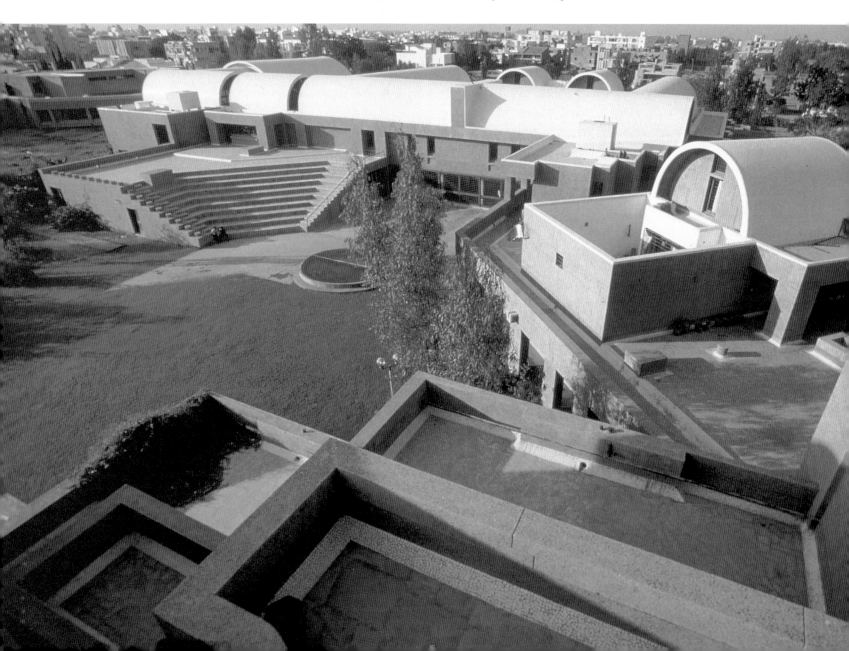

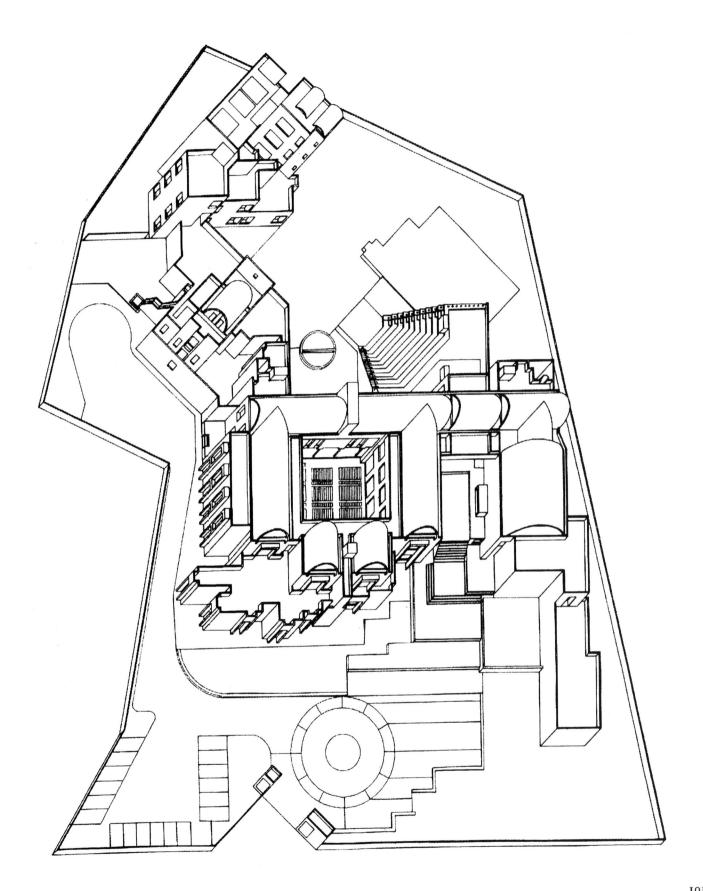

technically designated an exhibition space, effectively transfers the external experience of progression inside, even though the sudden gloom comes as something of a shock and this darkness is not relieved until reaching the arcade around the central court.

The court is the heart of the institute, signifying Doshi's observations over many years that 'architecture in a hot and dry climate has evolved as a dual system of structuring one main system to support the activity areas and another to support the envelope which protects the inside'. This duality of building within a building around a court is like the body and soul. Here the shell represents the body and the open court is its soul. The effect of slowly ascending onto a platform, through a long defile, down a generously scaled dark hall, and finally coming out into the light at the middle

level of this courtyard, is memorable and is a sequence the architect has controlled tightly. The shortest vaults, a pair over the offices near the front entrance, resemble sentinels when seen from the court arcade, or towers which protect its security. This kind of originality continues around each of the edges of the courtyard, the articulated rim where the human-made profile interacts with or locks into the sky – a configuration intended to inspire.

The duality of which Doshi speaks was a difficult metaphor to sustain in the residential wing. This includes the rector's residence and twenty living units, arranged ten to a floor, clustered behind it around a small triangular courtyard near the southern perimeter of the site. His answer has been to bring the two clusters into balance. While the courtyard was created

**Left and below**  The entrance is approached by a series of steps and terraces. The vaults, like those at Sangath, are covered by glazed ceramic pieces, although here the buildings stand higher. Again, water is an important feature, descending from a misting fountain that helps to cool the air nearby.

Facing south across the amphitheatre.

to be a geometrically ordered replica of nature, the symbolically appropriate core of the Institute, nature itself becomes the focal point of its residential component. The open-air amphitheatre, a favourite component in many of Doshi's designs (such as the National Institute of Fashion Technology in Delhi, 1997) sets up a diagonal axis which opposes the approach from the main gate to the entrance at the northeastern edge of this natural mirror image. As the outdoor replica of the indoor auditorium, it is attached to the demising wall that separates the main building from its outdoor garden and is positioned to respond visually to the housing cluster across the lawn. Land forms have been subtly manipulated to create a bowl-shaped perimeter around the garden, with slopes carefully planted to establish a feathery green fringe. If and when expansion occurs, it will intentionally fill in the area between the outdoor auditorium and the contours of the hill, keeping the concept of the bowl intact.

The housing cluster presents as much of a surprise as the serenity of the courtyard in the interior of the Institute. Doshi has turned what could easily have become a design liability, or extraneous foil that draws energy and attention away from the strong centre, into an advantage that both enhances the centre and inversely echoes it.

Internal courts, recessed window openings, deep eaves and balconies
all bring shade to the surfaces of the building.

107

# GANDHI LABOUR INSTITUTE

**Below** Section and elevations.

**Opposite** Inside the central courtyard.

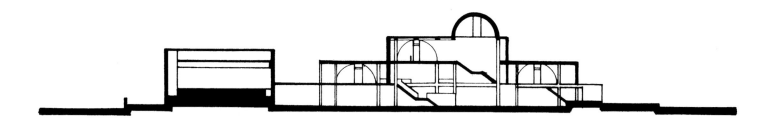

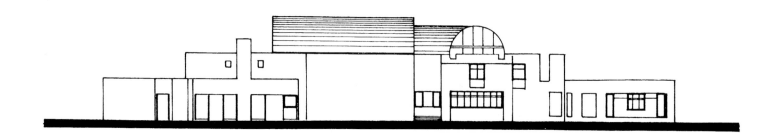

Terraces in the stacked housing units overlook the gardens.

The units are clustered around a small interior court, but the garden itself is their interior world, an intention that is symbolized by a circular pool near the amphitheatre. It is bisected with neatly clipped grass on the half facing the Institute and water in the half facing the residences, the solid and liquid characteristics of their respective references implied in the diversion.

The staircase to all levels of the stacked housing units, which step up in terraces to encourage sitting outdoors overlooking the garden and Institute below, has been vertically accentuated and painted white to differentiate it from the grey stone of the housing it serves. This straightforward measure allows the tower effectively to terminate the diagonal line set up by the outdoor amphitheatre, allowing this entire cluster to hold its own visually. Even though it is far smaller in scale than the Institute itself, the housing cluster has the presence to act as a fitting coda for the dynamic the architect has established. Original sketches and models show an intention to use vaulted roofs here also, but these were finally subdued to take advantage of the massed strength of flat cornices.

The Gandhi Institute and Sangath were designed at the same time and the similarities are not coincidental. Doshi's village origins are recalled in each; the smaller scale of Sangath necessitated a concentration of the ideas used in the Institute one and a half kilometres

away. Once understood as abstracted replications of a traditional community, each may then be interpreted as idealized proposals for a new language, a new order. The individual vaults each represent a house cluster around the village square, whose green replaces the farmers' fields. The vault, created with cone-shaped clay plugs manually covered with a thin layer of concrete in which pieces of broken china were embedded, was also intended as a prototype. The resulting composite construction is inexpensive, remarkably strong yet light, and environmentally intelligent, with the mud contributing high thermal mass and the white ceramic surface providing high reflectivity. India is one of the few countries that can still provide the labour-intensive handicraft required to create these vaults and, without making value judgments about the prevailing wage rates that make such exquisite finishes possible, Doshi feels it is the architect's responsibility in India to originate new ways to use crafts such as this, to perpetuate skills and transform them.

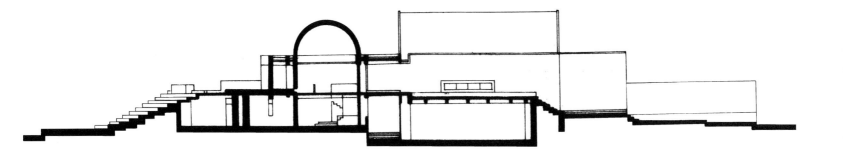

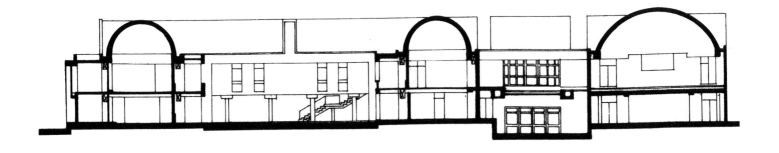

**Top** Section showing amphitheatre steps, cross-section and section of vaulted buildings (two sides of the main court). The entrance approach is at first floor level. The section also shows the progression from single to triple-height volumes.

**Bottom** Section through the buildings around the main courtyard. The main entrance level is right of centre, between two vaulted sections.

**Opposite** Amphitheatre steps (**left**) and entrance steps (**right**).

# 8

# Aranya Low-Cost Housing, *Indore, 1983–86*

Housing shortages in India, particularly in urban areas, where nearly 23 per cent of the population of well over 800 million now live, are a severe problem. Well intentioned efforts by the government in the recent past have generally consisted of attempts to provide ready-built dwellings for the poor, but the time required to build them and their relatively high cost have made ready-built houses untenable in the long run, leading to attempts to upgrade slums and to provide serviced sites for new housing development. The 'sites and services' scheme allows people to buy a lot with sewer, electricity and water connections provided at a minimal cost. Materials to construct a house may be purchased from a co-operative, and repaid over time. Incrementally planned house designs are usually preferred by the co-operative to ensure the economic advantages of pre-fabrication and standardization as well as formal cohesion, to encourage a sense of community. Since few purchasers have construction skills, 'sites and services' schemes also provide training programmes to teach buyers building techniques.

Indore, a commercial centre in the state of Madhya Pradesh, is typical of urban areas throughout India in that it suffers from acute housing shortages and poor infrastructure distribution. The Aranya Community Housing Project, located six kilometres from the centre

Housing at the Aranya Community Project: seeking a community character by establishing harmony between people and the built environment. The streets, wide enough for the movement of small traffic (**opposite**), become narrower (**above**) as they penetrate the residential heart of the township, imitating the scale and security of a village community.

of Indore on the Agra–Bombay Highway, is the result of a series of studies initiated by Doshi in the early 1980s. Through his Vastu-Shilpa Foundation, he has constantly carried out research on the dynamics of squatter settlements to determine the hidden order

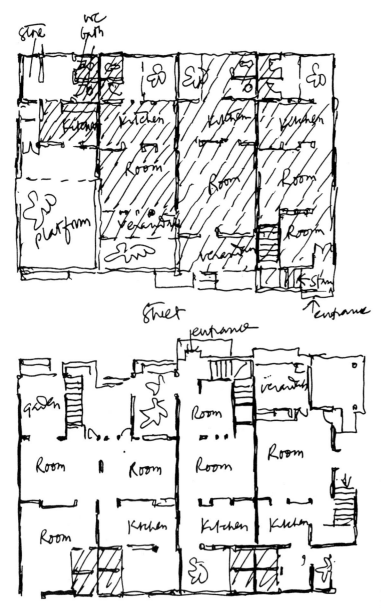

beneath what ordinarily appears to be a chaotic jumble of ramshackle dwellings. He found that the slums in the area, while unplanned and crowded, had a legible pattern, with huts clustered into small neighbourhoods and houses with public zones opening onto common spaces. Small shops were present in even the poorest settlements, as was 'landscaping', with trees often planted in public areas. Streets are not just for pedestrian or vehicular traffic but are also the preferred setting for social, economic and domestic activities.

Provision of utilities, however, is a chronic problem in squatter settlements, a critical missing component for a healthy community.

In 1983, Doshi was formally commissioned to plan a township by the Indore Development Authority, and the extensive Vastu-Shilpa studies of the economic and territorial factors that form squatter settlements came into play. The project, comprising about 6,500 housing units built primarily for the 'economically weaker sector', or poor, but also including other income groups, has been planned to grow to house 40,000. Doshi's original premise was that a viable community is more than an assembly of well designed and well built homes and must also involve public and private agencies working in tandem to provide a secure financial basis so that the community can become firmly established. Aranya depends on 'material banks' that the residents can draw upon at various stages of improvement, and training centres to teach construction skills, as well as the provision of infrastructure which relies on the assistance of outside agencies for financial support. Seeking maximum efficiency, support facilities to enable construction during the initial intensive building phase were planned to convert to permanent industries to sustain the community after the majority of construction was completed.

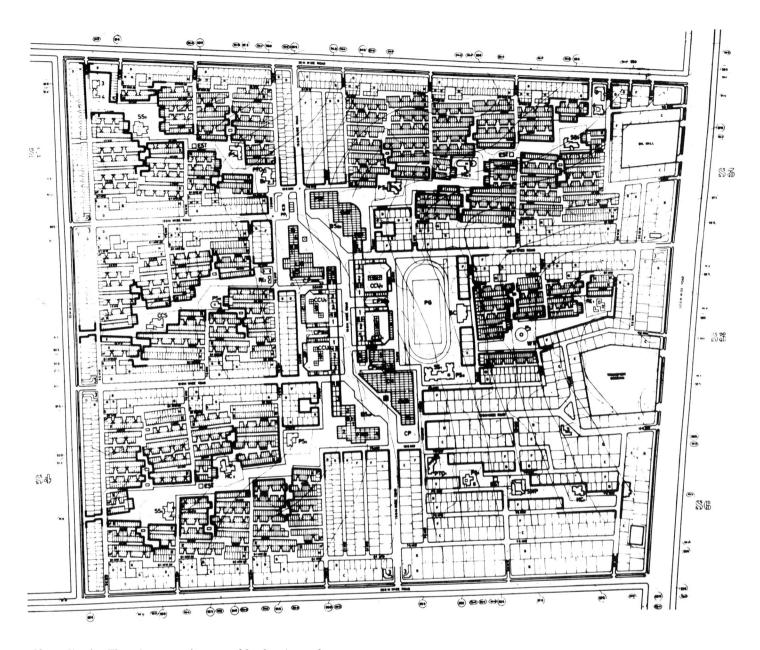

**Above** Site plan. The main street, at the centre of the plan, zig-zags from top to bottom, breaking the asymmetrical, irregular grid. Zoned housing is arranged in clusters around the main service cores.

**Opposite** Doshi's preliminary sketches show sensitivity to the need for outside space within a limited area.

**Top and bottom left** Housing densities in Indian towns.

**Top and bottom right** Photograph and model showing density of Aranya Housing Project.

**Opposite** Serviced sites before construction (**below**) and a constructed street (**above**).

Climate and site conditions at Indore presented the architect with a major challenge, since Madhya Pradesh has a hot, dry climate with scant vegetation. In the winter, from December to February, the climate is cool and dry with a mean temperature of 5 degrees centigrade and relative humidity of 68 per cent. In summer, from April to June, temperatures rise to about 25 degrees centigrade with relative humidity of 90 per cent. The rainy season begins in July and continues through September, with a mean annual rainfall of 882 millimetres. The Aranya site is flat, with a natural rainwater channel running diagonally across it towards the southwest corner. The lack of topographical

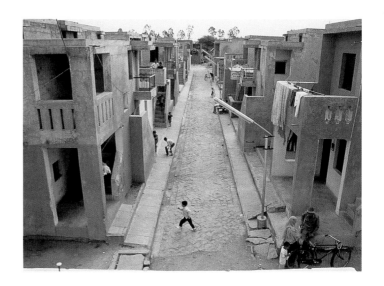

features to respond to helped Doshi focus on the climate and the residents as the key factors in his design, as he set out four general objectives for Aranya. These are: (1) to create a township where a sense of continuity and fundamental values of security exist in a good living environment; (2) to achieve a community character by establishing harmony between the built environment and the people; (3) to create a balanced community of various socio-economic groups, encouraging co-operation, tolerance and self-help generated through a physical planning process; and (4) to evolve a framework through design, where incremental physical development can take place within legal, economic and organizational guidelines.

Doshi's four objectives are not merely rhetorical since the population of Aranya is a mixture of Hindu, Muslim, Christian, Sikh, Buddhist and Jain. Doshi's stipulation of providing a viable socio-economic balance in the community was also imaginatively implemented by mixing income levels. By 1983, self-help site-and-service housing was no longer a novel concept but Doshi's provision of construction facilities that can be converted to light industry to provide employment for residents indicates that an additional dimension of planning is involved. The mixture of income levels is another such provision. Rather than merely providing a balanced social mix, higher-priced

plots for upper-income buyers have been provided to supply a cross-subsidy for the lower-income properties to lower the loan repayments for disadvantaged families. Surplus funds, or amounts paid over the average plot cost, are held in common trust, to be used to assist the poorest families in building their homes. Families make downpayments based on their average income, contributing monthly payments on the balance. Service charges for electricity and water are also scaled to income level.

The specific design approach that Doshi used was to divide the 86-hectare site with a north–south spine where the main amenities are clustered, feeding three zones of housing on each side. He offset both the spine and the main pedestrian streets leading into each sector to prevent the visual monotony that gridded plans can produce. The choice of orientation, as well as the use of offsets, also maximizes shade. The higher buildings, containing shops, offices, cottage industries and some housing, serve as walls along the main spine, keeping it in shade most of the day, except when the sun is directly overhead. The narrow lanes between rows of houses, the ends of which have been kept to a minimum, alternate with the larger pedestrian lanes, used mainly by bicycles and motor scooters. Houses in the residential districts have been clustered in groups of ten, separated by open spaces which join the pedestrian spines. A septic tank has been provided for every two clusters, and water is drawn from three local reservoirs to serve the entire project. Rather than being regarded as a pragmatic necessity, the service cores were considered the key to this sites-and-services scheme, the 'nuclei' around which the houses, which can take many different configurations, can grow.

Doshi was sensitive to the fact that the success or failure of the community revolved around the efficiency and ease of maintenance of these services and that 'the service core and the supporting infrastructure became the critical elements of the design.' To ensure thoroughness of attention to such components, and to the residential units, which the architect feels are the most important elements to the people themselves, Doshi adopted a comprehensive rather than sequential approach, to avoid treating the houses as the 'residue' of the master planning framework, unable to change. Rather than focusing on the system, his emphasis was to concentrate on the residents. This is evident in myriad details throughout the project. One instance of this is the architect's attempt to promote a sense of community by enhancing street life, providing each house with an *otta*, or outdoor platform. An important feature of the traditional Indian house, the *otta* is a transitional zone, a meeting place literally located between the private residential world and the public realm. At Indore, these open platforms, similar to Arab *iwan,* are a critical part of the streetscape, allowing passers-by to stop and chat, thus maintaining community cohesiveness.

As built, the Aranya Housing scheme breaks down into 58 per cent residential use, 23.5 per cent pedestrian and vehicular access roads, 8 per cent open space, and 7 per cent shared community and commercial facilities. The 6,500 plots sold are divided into eleven types depending upon income level. The smallest, 35-square-metre plots for the economically weaker sector accounted for 66 per cent of the total, containing options of water tap only, water tap with bath, or water tap, bath and cooking space in addition to the basic site, plinth base and service core provided. House extensions, such as porches, balconies and open stairs, also contribute to the indoor-outdoor character of the house facades facing the pedestrian spine.

The lower-income group, making up 11 per cent of the community, is as uniformly distributed throughout each of the six sectors as the poorest group, while the middle-income group at 14 per cent and the high-income group at 9 per cent are each located along the arterial roads that line the periphery of the site along the north, west and south edges. The six sectors in the plan were viewed by Doshi as individual villages, each as 'viable, almost autonomous sub-communities' similar

to those found in the majority of Indian cities today, and the affordability of the lots for the poorest residents was critical to the project's success. Monthly loan repayments were determined through extensive research by the Vastu-Shilpa Foundation, which concluded that 'monthly incomes of the economically weaker sector are underestimated in the national statistics as they do not take into account the incomes from the informal economy.' Vastu-Shilpa also anticipated that once construction proceeded, residents would subsidize their income by subletting rooms. In 1983, loan repayments for a family earning RS200 a month were RS25, rising to RS80 for a family income of RS400 a month. By way of comparison, the salary range for the lower, middle and higher income groups was estimated at RS450–600, and RS1100–1800 respectively.

In a local report prepared for the Aga Khan Award for Architecture, which the Aranya Low-Cost Housing Scheme won in 1996, one observer expressed alarm at the prevalence of brokering on the project site, outside a one-block area defined by 80 demonstration houses designed and supervised by the architect. Although this was unsubstantiated with property brokers, this suggests a lack of community spirit in the project. In his interviews, the observer discovered that only 15 to 20 per cent of the original plot owners still held the plots originally allotted to them, with the resale price of

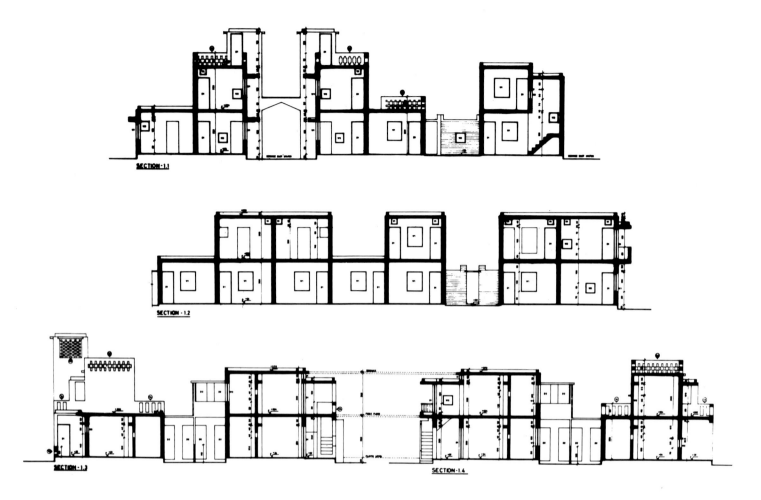

SECTION-1.1

SECTION - 1.2

SECTION-1.3          SECTION-1.4

plots averaging approximately ten times the original purchase price. This indicated that brokers were speculating that first-time buyers would be unable to pay the mortgages and would be forced to sell, the observer concluded. There are a number of critical multi-disciplinary inputs that are missing at Aranya. First, there is no evidence of any activity by non-governmental organizations concerned with community participation. Secondly, no identifiable arrangements for credit and mortgage had been put in place to enable slum dwellers to secure a plot. Thirdly, no arrangements for providing gainful employment had been made.

This last point contradicts the architect's intention of providing cottage industries for the community, evolving from the material and fabrication centres used during construction. It also prompts comparison with

Opposite Sections and photograph of housing units. The basic framework allows buildings to be extended in a legal, economical and planned way.

Below Terraces and balconies – open or sheltered, and at different heights – allow variation within the broad scheme. They also provide cool outdoor spaces.

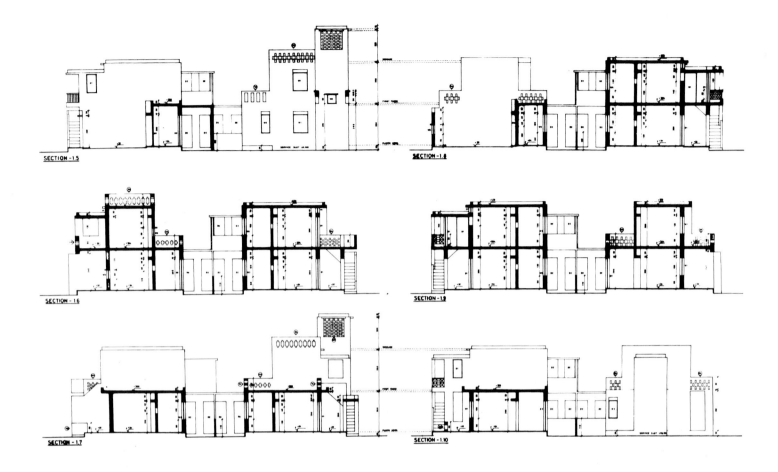

SECTION-1.5
SECTION-1.6
SECTION-1.6
SECTION-1.9
SECTION-1.7
SECTION-1.10

other examples, such as the Grameen Bank project in Bangladesh, a bold and effective attempt to allow low-income groups to build homes, begun by Mohammed Yunus in 1976. Dr Yunus became aware of the extent of the shelter shortage among the landless poor, which represents 60 per cent of the Bangladeshi population, in his capacity as director of the Rural Economics Programme at Chittagong University in the early 1970s. He became involved in making personal loans, then amounting to no more than one hundred homeless families who were excluded from receiving bank loans because they lacked collateral, and found them to be reliable in repaying the loans. Believing their exclusion from the credit system to be morally untenable, considering the contribution by the poor to the national economy through agricultural labour and cottage industry, Yunus tried to convince local banks to change their practices. When they refused he began a

bank of his own, on the basis that all people, regardless of social position, deserve lives of dignity and the chance to care for themselves if they have the determination to do so.

Such commitment, rather than the usual standards of credit-worthiness, became Yunus's main criterion in loaning money. The only condition the Grameen Bank imposed was that loans would be to communal groups, rather than individuals, making it harder to default. Loans are also only made to women since Yunus found them to be more reliable than men in repayment. Participation in the programme is limited to families whose total assets do not exceed the market value of an acre of land in their area, and loans are restricted to groups of five families or more, from whom a chairperson, who will deal directly with the Bank, is elected. Each loan is given for one year and paid back in weekly instalments with 5 per cent held aside to

**Opposite** Sections of housing units, showing creative use of inside and outside spaces.

**Below** Plan of first floor level. Circled figures above and below the plan indicate sections, such as 1.3, 1.5 and 1.7 illustrated opposite. Some of the other numbered sections correspond to those on p. 122.

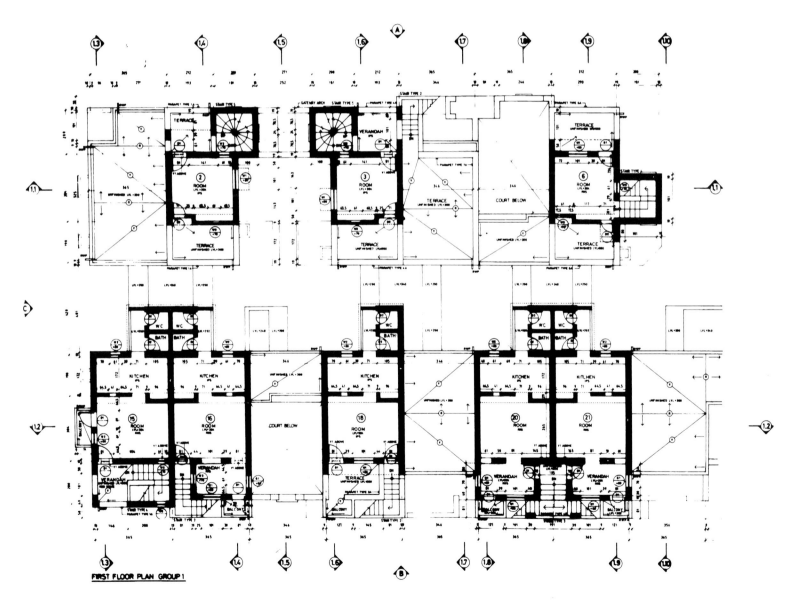

FIRST FLOOR PLAN GROUP 1

**Above and opposite**  Pair of show houses, before and after occupation.

**Right**  The space between housing clusters encourages social interaction, just as in a traditional narrow street of a typical urban district.

assist any member in difficulty, with group consent.

Within five years of its founding in 1983, the same year as the Aranya project was begun, the Grameen Bank had 535,170 participants in 11,793 villages throughout Bangladesh, and the loan recovery rate averaged 98.35 per cent. The Grameen Programme only offers two types of house, with the bank providing the components for each. The smaller house is 20 square metres, made up of four prefabricated reinforced concrete columns at each corner of a rectangular concrete slab, with a prefabricated latrine, and a corrugated metal roof, leaving residents to supply enclosing walls and partitions, which are typically of jute. The large house is similar with a bigger slab size. Aside from providing the columns, corrugated iron sheets, latrine and slab, the bank does not get involved in siting, subsidiary materials or the internal organization of the house.

The startling differences between the Aranya and Grameen models are an object lesson in how easy it is for good intentions to go astray; to allow architectural considerations to outweigh an awareness of social dynamics, regardless of the amount of physical research undertaken. In the Grameen Bank model, the lender realized that there is strength in numbers, and that the poor, having little experience in dealing with loans, may occasionally find it difficult to make payments on time. The lender also acknowledged the crucial role that women play in maintaining family cohesiveness and in financial planning, since they typically have the ingenuity required to stretch a meagre income to cover the basic necessities for survival. The Grameen house models are also neither overly complex nor too descriptive. The observer mentioned earlier concluded:

> The Aranya project is based on good intentions in which the innocence of the professional designers is symbolized in the 80 demonstration houses. If only slum resettlement projects were simply architectural problems capable of being overcome with good design. The river of poverty in India erodes such good intentions, if they are not safeguarded with innovations which can take the project through one decade.

The important lesson that the Aranya project has to offer, then, is that it is extremely difficult to provide housing for the poor that will actually develop all of the intricate networks of social, religious and economic characteristics of a true community and perpetuate these over time. This issue of appropriate design continues to be a critical point of debate in architectural and planning circles in India and in governments worldwide, with important implications for other developing nations and the post-industrial world. Doshi has an important place in this debate because of his long association with city-planning issues, beginning with his involvement in Chandigarh between 1956 and 1966. The most common criticism levelled at Le Corbusier's plans for Chandigarh is that in spite of all efforts to modify the formal language of Western modern architecture towards specific vernacular forms, the attempt by one architect to establish a new city is itself presumptuous given the multi-layered complications of the urban organism. The fine balance that is typically found in traditional settlements has increasingly been shown to be impervious to master planning and statistics, and even seems to resist incremental steps put forward by planners today as an alternative, or the zoning revisions being promoted by the new urbanists to create new towns in the image of the villages of the past. There

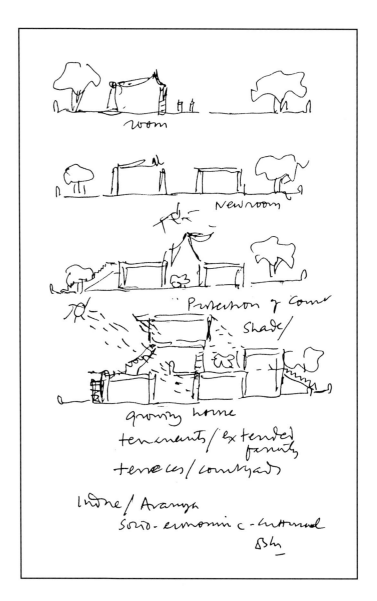

A preliminary sketch for the Aranya project indicates four stages in the natural growth of a house on a single site. The handwritten notes read as follows: 'room – new room – Protection of court – Shade – growing house – tenements/extended family – terraces/courtyards – Indore/Aranya – socio-economic-cultural – Doshi'

were undeniably significant breakthroughs at Chandigarh, such as the detached roof on the high court, serving as a natural extension of the parasol concept (demonstrated at Fatehpur Sikri). It was extremely advanced as an environmental statement, profoundly affecting Doshi's other mentor, Louis Kahn, in his design for the Assembly Building in Dacca, Bangladesh, a decade later. What Le Corbusier did, with Doshi's help, was to recognize the power of the sun in this context; sunstroke can kill after extended unprotected exposure. The roof of the high court is shaped like an aeroplane wing to encourage natural ventilation through the building beneath it. It is also separated from the building to absorb solar radiation while keeping it away from the main structure. This highly sophisticated approach to the positive use of climatic forces later led Kahn to 'wrap ruins' around the Assembly Building in Dacca to provide shade, and to prevent solar infiltration and glare. The Chandigarh High Court and Dacca Assembly Building are two rare instances of environmental consciousness in modern architecture, but significant as they are, they do not offset the arrogance of the assumption that cities such as Chandigarh and Dacca can be built in the first place.

One year after Aranya was commissioned, Doshi began studies for Vidyadhar Nagar, a satellite community for the city of Jaipur in Rajasthan.

It was intended as an 'energy-conscious' alternative to the Chandigarh prototype, with which it shares many recognizable features. Like Chandigarh, it begins with a square perimeter and a strong north–south, east–west cross axis along which major communal and institutional functions are located, using the same logic about blocking the sun that is found at Aranya.

# 9
## Husain-Doshi Gufa, *1992–95*

The Gufa, which is a collaborative effort between Doshi and the Indian artist M. F. Husain, began as an art gallery for the exhibition of the artist's work. It undeniably represents an anomaly in Doshi's *oeuvre*, a natural and free expressionistic essay that differs completely from the rigorous order evident in Doshi's previous work. This dramatic departure cannot be entirely explained by the artist's influence, but rather marks a sea-change in Doshi's work in general, also marked by the 'stories' or narratives that now accompany each new project. The traditional heritage of these narratives echoes the deeper historical resonance of the projects themselves.

The references for the Gufa are elemental and primeval: the cave, the circle, the mountain, the breast, and historical precedents in India itself which emerge from these universal prototypes, the Buddhist *stupa* (memorial) and its appearance in the cave monasteries of Karli and Ajanta in particular. The *stupa*, as the primary reference, has a dual significance as both the tomb of Buddha and the symbol of the pursuit of knowledge, one of his 'four noble truths'.

**Left** Extraordinary yet natural forms express Doshi's exploration of deeper cultural associations. Glazed ceramic mosaic reflects glare and heat.

**Right** Street shrine to Shiva, Ahmedabad, with decorative ceramic mosaic covering the dome.

In recognition of humanity's responsibilities and ability to teach itself, the *stupa* formally signifies and implies the enlightening nature of knowledge, the reference to a source of light also relating to Louis Kahn's mystical belief in the life-giving qualities of this element and its importance as more than a space-defining substance in architecture. Originally, *stupas* varied in shape from the prevalent hemisphere to pyramids and cones and were often 'covered from top to bottom with small triangular recesses for oil lamps, so that the whole monument could be illuminated and appeared as one huge, radiating dome of light'.[10] The use of light to enhance its dome-like shape also emphasized the sky vault, as

**Opposite and above left** Chaitya hall (Cave 8), Karli, first century. The stupa is a monolithic domed drum, positioned at the end of the hall. The teak ribs of the vaulted roof are set into the rock.

**Above right** Pair of stupas with inverted stepped finials, Ajanta Caves.

well as the life cycle of 'destruction and creation, death and birth'.[11] In this way, it captured the essence of the Buddhist philosophy of regeneration.

As Buddhism became more entrenched and powerful in India, the *stupa* form evolved with the growth of the religion it came to symbolize. The key to its universal appeal was its primary associations and its ability to assimilate pre-existing tangible images which

were transformed as they were incorporated into it. In Gandhara, for example, the Indian *stupa* was merged with the funerary tumulus on a square pedestal to become a singularly regional terrace *stupa* with columns, pilasters, entablatures, and niches added as a holdover from the Alexandrian community that had settled in the area during the Macedonian king's campaign in Bacria during the Hellenistic period.[12]

The *stupa* has communal rather than individual references, and its rounded shape suggests eternity and envelopment, focusing the attention of an entire society on its group identity and structure.[13] It represents the unity of the community, as well as the unity of body and mind that is essential in the spiritual training of Buddhism.

The main difference between the Gufa and the *stupa*, of course, is that the 25-millimetre thin ferrocement shell that has been used as the structure of Doshi's museum, as well as the sloping columns that support it internally, convert solid into hollow, extending the reference further to the Buddhist caves at Ajanta and Ellora. The Ajanta caves are among the most important archaeological, religious sites in India. Architectural and iconic evolution over several

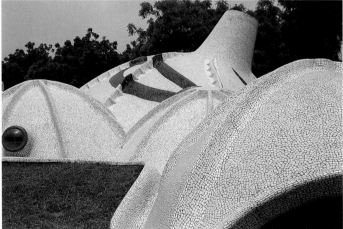

**Above**  The entrance is approached down a flight of steps into the cave-like interior.

**Left and opposite**  '…on some of the shells, there appeared snouts with apertures, trying to capture perhaps fresh air or light…' Doshi, 'The Revelation'

**Opposite** Site plan. Entrances are approached by steps (upper left and lower right of the plan). The underground vaults are supported by pillars.

**Below** The domes conceal an underground network of caves, which were designed as a combined gallery and residence for the artist M. F. Husain.

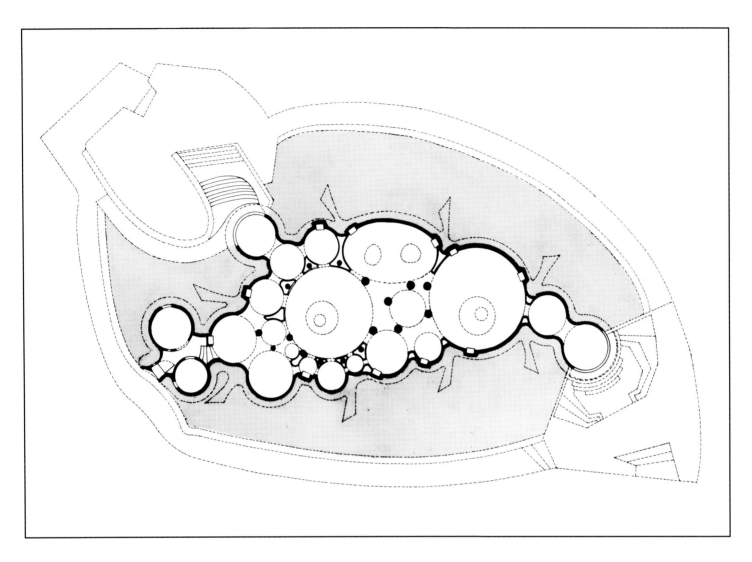

centuries have been preserved in stone, making it a petrified textbook. At the time the cave temples were begun, in the second century AD, Ajanta was on a main pilgrimage and trade route, explaining why the cave complex is so large, since it housed resident monks, as well as providing lodging for pilgrims. Since early *stupa*s contained artifacts connected with Buddha, those in the caves would have been important objects of pilgrimage in their own right. The caves were excavated over a period of 300 years about 250 feet above ground level in an almost perpendicular rock escarpment that curves around in a semicircle. Archaeologists have numbered each of the twenty-nine caves sequentially, beginning from the southeast, even though some are unfinished and each varies in size.[14] Some are *viharas*, or Buddhist monasteries, and others are *chaityas*, or worship halls, usually containing the *stupa*. The *viharas* of Ajanta are typically centralized and symmetrical. Cave 1, for example, is an impressive *vihara* containing decoratively carved pillars with brackets and sculptural figures and a long processional frieze below the cornice, as well as wall paintings of religious stories and Indian myths. Such themes are repeated throughout many of the other twenty-eight caves.

In addition to the Ajanta caves, the Karli temple in Maharashtra state, on the west coast of India on the Arabian Sea, is another obvious precedent for the Husain-Doshi Gufa.

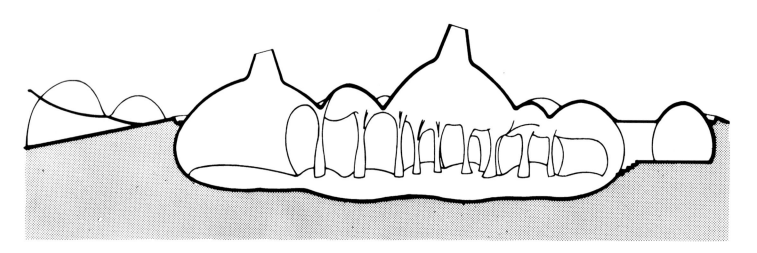

Originally established as a Buddhist temple during the Kshatrapas Dynasty around 100 AD, the *chaitya* hall, carved out of the stone side of a mountain, is 130 feet long, 50 feet wide and 50 feet high, requiring an estimated 325,000 cubic feet of rock to be removed to create it. While it has the same symmetrical layout as many of the Ajanta temples, the Karli *chaitya* is larger and more carefully scaled. The central hall is supported by two rows of columns which divide the interior into a wider central aisle and two side aisles. The columns have octagonal shafts which are wide at the base and taper toward the capital. The capitals are pairs of elephants, each mounted with embracing couples. The ribs, which span from column line to column line, create the vaulted roof of the cave, and the focus of the

hall is a large *stupa*, transformed from its Buddhist associations to a representation of the Hindu deity Shiva. It is a large circular stone drum covered by a heavy dome surmounted by an inverted finial and a delicately carved teak umbrella. The entry facade of the temple is ornately carved, and a large horseshoe-shaped doorway echoes the shape of the plan of the inner hall.

The Karli temple conforms to the ancient Hindu *Shastras*, compiled by priests over many centuries. These give specific guidelines for building design that conforms with the environment, so that it achieves harmony with the natural elements of sun, sky, water, earth and air. Complex calculations involving geometry, astrology and philosophy indicate orientation and dimensions.

In a story written about the Gufa, 'The Revelation', Doshi weaves a complex network of sources of inspiration, including a grove of neem trees, which he mentions as being described in the *Ayurveda* as a 'wonder tree', a vision of interconnected tortoises with different-sized shells and mouths opening in different directions, and the legend of Kurmaavatar, Lord Vishnu's reincarnation.[15]

Doshi refers to Ronchamp as 'seminal' in Le Corbusier's career, but it was also a dramatic point of departure from the rationalistic principles that had established his reputation as a founder of the Modern movement. What amazed critics and admirers alike in the new expressionistic direction that Ronchamp represented was Le Corbusier's capacity for passion.

'What is unexpected is the experience inside. Are you not surprised to find that it is larger than you had imagined and deceptive in its forms? The skylights that you had seen on the roof as protuberances are not immediately visible, yet the light that they let in makes the Gufa space glow, lending it an almost ethereal quality.'
Doshi, 'The Revelation'

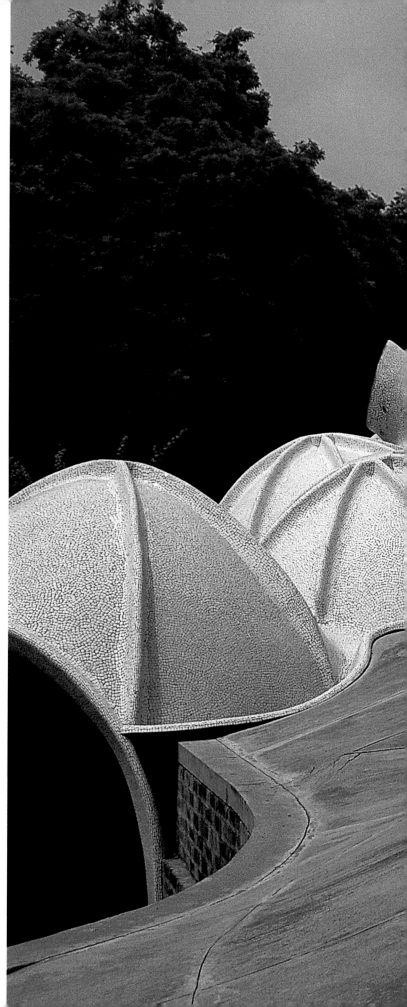

'A building which is dynamic, difficult to describe yet great to experience.
… In technological terms, it should challenge all the usual conventions of
architecture, be made of simple materials but should show how to be natural…
In short, start afresh, forget that you are an architect and design this building
using your innermost sensibility. Become and be part of the process
rather than an outsider.'
Doshi, 'The Revelation'

It was as if he realized that artistic release and emotion were too important to be continually excluded and that the time had come to change direction.

'The Revelation' also strongly indicates an important shift in career direction for Doshi. The previously rational balance between Western and indigenous influence is deliberately tipped here toward a deeper cultural exploration. This exploration goes beyond formal references to include the way the Gufa was made, a compelling combination of high technology and traditional techniques that also describes the essential timelessness of technology itself. Ironically, the methods used to construct this building, which touches such primal chords, were reliant on computer-aided programmes and complicated concrete-shell engineering, putting it clearly into that new category of structure exemplified by Frank Gehry's Guggenheim Museum in Bilbao, Spain, which could not have been conceived without computer visualization and representation. Yet like the Guggenheim, the construction of the Gufa was finally dependent upon the innate skill and knowledge of local builders who had to translate highly sophisticated diagrams into reality. Doshi speaks of the *adivasis*, or 'tribals', who felt they were reliving the ancient ritual of Pithora Bava while building the museum, an intriguing reminder of the timeless connection between tradition and technology. The composition of the 25-millimetre shell is a physical parallel with this link, handmade from reinforcing bars and mesh buttered with cement. The concrete was then covered with a compacted layer of vermiculite followed by a mosaic of pieces of broken china using a technique similar to that seen on the dome of a small street shrine to Shiva in Ahmedabad. The use of the coating, as well as depressing the gallery more than a metre into the ground, is an effective insulating strategy and the white tiles also reflect the suns rays, helping to keep the interior cool. The protuberances of which Doshi dreamt finally emerged as porthole windows, specifically oriented to let in the maximum amount of light and minimum amount of heat, giving the interior a golden glow. To enhance the cave-like feeling of the gallery, the contours of the site were retained, rather than being levelled. The gently undulating surface of the earth can still be perceived beneath the thin concrete floor slab poured over it.

'The protuberances on the surfaces perhaps remind you of telescopes or the bulging eyes of the chameleons, crocodiles or the frogs. As you will observe tonight, they will act as torches and their positions will so light the surrounding trees and landscape that it will appear as if it is a moonscape. ...the hundred and one neem trees that surround this new Gufa protect the place as if it is a paradise.' Doshi, 'The Revelation'

**Left** M. F. Husain (far left) and Balkrishna Doshi (far right).

# The Revelation

Yes, like you, there have been many visitors who have asked me about the origin of this concept. So I have decided to describe to you all the events that have affected the concept, design, construction, and architecture of the Husain-Doshi Gufa.

It was in 1962 that Louis Kahn first came to Ahmedabad. During this brief visit, I took him to the Ahmedabad Education Society's campus where the School of Architecture was to be located. I was the architect of the campus, and the entire site was full of lush green, large mango trees. There were more than 45 of these. Underneath one grove, there were huts where the AES staff lived.

On seeing these, Lou remarked that humility and simple directness are great virtues and if we could achieve these in our buildings, they would then become architecture. Unfortunately, all those mango trees are now no more. They say that the mango trees are sensitive to vibrations caused by human activity. Anyway, as a mark of respect to those grand ancient trees, I planted neem trees in the same locations. As you know, even neem is described in the ayurveda as a wonder tree, beneficial in many ways.

After Lou's visit I began to reflect on his remark and visited the site at odd hours. Without realizing, the frequency of my visits increased as my fascination to watch all that occurred grew, and I tried to listen to the vibration and activities that lay deep in her womb. The earth always rekindles many dormant ideas in me. I feel happy when the earth itself provides me with clues for a solution to the design. The buildings at the CEPT campus that you see today are my responses to those vibrations and the clues I have gathered at the site. All those who work and visit the campus always wish to return. They do so, perhaps, to respond to the mother earth's calling.

Somehow, affinity to land made Husain speak to me about an underground building almost twenty years ago at Gunvantbhai's residence. Even though we discussed this for climatic reasons, I did not give it a serious thought until I designed Sangath in 1980. It was then that I remembered Kahn, Husain and the design of open floor at lower level in the School of Architecture building surrounded by hills which appears to many as a basement.

Fascinated by this sudden co-relation between Kahn's remarks on direct, yet well proportioned design, and Husain's questions to dig deep in ground to avoid the heat, I again roamed around the campus site as if it had cast some sort of a spell on me. As usual, I watched the neem trees that I had planted in place of the mango trees, and kind of waited for their response.

One late evening it was very calm, and it so happened that one of the oldest neem trees next to the present Gufa site began to sway purposefully, as if to call my attention. As soon as I noticed this unusual swaying of one single tree, I went near it and sat down next to its trunk. Gradually, the tree calmed down and as if to focus my attention to a particular *spot, dropped a branch from its foliage. Strangely, it is the same location where the Gufa presently stands. Shocked by this rather unusual happening, I picked up the branch and, no sooner had I held the fallen branch in my hands, my entire body began to vibrate as if I was a diviner.*

*I still vividly remember that Saturday evening. It was quiet and getting dark. I was sitting down on this lonely spot with the branch in my hands. Then after about a minute, I felt a powerful pull from deep within the earth, a sensation I had never ever experienced before. Taking this as a sign of something very unusual about to happen, I closed my eyes. Immediately, there appeared a body of a large tortoise-like form. Unlike the normal tortoise, this was long and had two large mouths facing each other at the opposite ends. They were interconnected with many shells of different shapes and sizes. It had six legs and in their manner and positions appeared to be attempting to somehow move. Yet I did not clearly notice any movement.*

*Anyway, on some of the shells, there appeared a few snouts with apertures trying to capture perhaps fresh air or light. I tried to comprehend this strange image and even tried to relate it to the legend of the Kurmaavatar, one of Lord Vishnu's reincarnation. I had this strange feeling that it was trying to convey some message from the ancient mango trees through this neem branch I was holding but I was unable to fathom. I returned home rather perplexed and wondered why this vision and why to me? This took place almost eight years*

M. F. Husain (centre) and Balkrishna Doshi (right).

'One late evening it was very calm, and it so happened that one of the oldest neem trees began to sway purposefully, as if to call my attention… Gradually the tree calmed down and as if to focus my attention to a particular spot, dropped a branch from its foliage. … I picked up the branch, and no sooner had I held the fallen branch in my hands, my entire body began to vibrate as if I was a diviner. … I felt a powerful pull from deep within the earth, a sensation I had never ever experienced before. … now on seeing the Gufa, built in reality, I perceive its real connection.'
Doshi, 'The Revelation'

ago and now on seeing the Gufa, built in reality, I now perceive its real connection.

Two years ago, Husain paid a sudden visit to Gunvantbhai and recalled his earlier discussions of the underground building. He asked me where he could find a small piece of land for building an art gallery to exhibit his works. After visiting several places, I took him to meet Piraji Sagara at the AES Campus and he persuaded Husain to agree to this site for his new gallery. After completing the normal formalities with Shrenikbhai Kasturbhai and members of the Governing Body of AES, Husain formally asked me to design an underground building which he called the Gufa. He also emphasized that this Gufa should become a demonstration of a positive collaboration between a painter and an architect.

On returning to the office, I was again struck by the particular selection of the site because it was here that I had the vision of this pre-historic Kurma eight years ago. Somehow, I ignored the coincidences and continued conceptualizing the designs for the Gufa. But even after many months, I could not arrive at any clear image except that the Gufa, as the name suggests, has to be underground, and perhaps, without a definite form. The issue of providing natural light, an entrance to lower level as well as structural system and materials to be used were not at all thought of.

At this juncture, a Canadian architect, Lise Trottier, came to work in my studio. We discussed various ways of designing an artist's underground gallery. As mythical examples, she mentioned the Loch Ness monster and the Stone Henge. I talked about my experiences of the Ajanta caves, the Kailash temple and the caves I had seen at Mount Abu. However, none of these examples seemed right for a present-day Gufa. So we were not getting anywhere. When things don't seem to work, I usually leave them alone. I have realized that they do resurface and only when an appropriate response is ready.

After a long time, again coincidentally on a Saturday, I visited the site to find a clue and that night, I had a dream. The same Kurma appeared before my eyes and began to ask me questions about my present approach to architecture and its relevance to contemporary times as well as to the teachings of my guru Le Corbusier. What was shocking were the questions. They were the same questions that Le Corbusier had asked, especially during the last decade of his career and during the designing of the Chapel at Ronchamp. I then realized that with the passing of the years, I had ignored them as too esoteric.

Noticing my hesitation in answering the questions, Kurma asked me how I would define architecture – in its deepest sense. Having lost the habit, I could not offer any clear answer. My definitions emphasized only the contemporary and day to day notions of how to design an acceptable form, or create a well lit functional space, or employ construction technologies available within the means etc. etc.

Kurma nodded its heads in disapproval and began to speak of the deeper, profound goals and pursuits in architecture.

Kurma reminded me of the discoveries made by Giulio Romano and others during the post-Renaissance and Baroque period. He emphasized how the definition of space and form were gradually being dissolved, three-dimensionally, and how the sky was becoming part of the interior space. He even talked about optical illusions and scooping of a solid mass into continuous layered elements as in Kailash temple at Ellora and how they are essential to make us realize that the space and form that we see are part of the infinite, and hence timeless and illusory.

Then he reminded me of my sojourn at Le Corbusier's studio and the design of the Chapel at Ronchamp where Le Corbusier has skilfully restated the issues raised by the earlier masters in contemporary terms. I then recalled my visit to the Chapel and my experiences on seeing the fluidity of the spaces and forms which no one so far has been able to either describe or photograph. And the exhilaration I had felt.

I was shocked that in course of my rather busy practice, satisfied with marginal innovations, I had forgotten the lessons of Ronchamp, my guru's most seminal masterpiece. I immediately realized that in true architecture one must experience joys and celebrations. It must affect our inner self. It cannot be distinguished separately either as modulation of light or surfaces or supporting system. On the contrary, a good design merges floors, walls, ceilings into one contiguous whole and creates an organic space almost like a living being. What it encompasses within and without its surfaces are the voids which generate energy. This energy then reduces all stresses within all the elements that surround this object which we call architecture. The total environment then emanates peace and tranquillity. Even the air becomes calm yet vital. It then becomes a small universe, a microcosm, we can call paradise.

As I began to explain this experience at the Chapel to Kurma, he smiled and then I could very clearly see the image of the Kurma I had seen eight years ago. Then I saw that it had a very thin tenuous skin covered with white, shiny surface. The modulation of this skin was complex due to the intermingling of many rounded shapes of varied heights, dimensions and inclinations. On these dome-like structures, there appeared protrusions almost like apertures in a bunker trying to track celestial objects. They were all pointed in different directions. There were two domes which were raised indicating the possible entrances. Since there was no way to enter, I searched from above and decided that the interior must be very fluid and continuous. The entire mass appeared to be almost mobile and suspended.

It struck me then why Kurma had talked about the Ronchamp Chapel and the Baroque experiments. Perhaps it was suggesting that I should not stick to a module or a height but combine the varied biological experiences into this design. However, not understanding fully the reasons for such an appearance at this stage, I asked Kurma as to what relevance it had for the Gufa at this site.

*Hearing that, Kurma said 'Doshi, do not get confused about dream and wakefulness because they are different only if seen through your personal lifetime. Viewed on a different scale, both are the same. Remember that form, space, structure, if you want them to last, should be integrated totally; so that the final object becomes a living being. Also, remember that as you progress, grow in your understanding of the universal governance, you will have the opportunity to combine the skills available from all your friends and colleagues such as engineers, contractors, masons, labourers, architects, clients, suppliers, etc. Because each one within him has an instinct which tells him about how life works. If you can take help from them without hindrance from your ego, you will be able to build architecture which is profound.'*

*Amazing as it sounds at this juncture, it then projected, like holograms, a series of egg-like forms, forms of fruits, forms of bones and mentioned that such forms do exist in nature and that man is capable of constructing them if he took the aid of the latest computers as well as the material technology.*

*Kurma continued, 'What this Gufa wants to be, is what you see in these forms: a building which is dynamic, difficult to describe yet great to experience. It must be a building to which everyone should be attracted. It must have places for children, for the old, for the common man as well as the elite. What it should do is to provide for the city, an example of a non-identifiable architecture, yet very meaningful and useful to all. It should also at the same time provide its master, Husain,*

Above M. F. Husain (left) and Balkrishna Doshi.

**Opposite above** '… hearing the chanting of Sheshnaga, Husain suddenly got up, held a large brush in his hand and climbed the domes. He feverishly painted in oil on the still-incomplete glazed domes a large cobra connecting the two large rotundas.'
Doshi, 'The Revelation'

**Opposite below** 'The columns, even though occurring at random and of varied thickness, some at an inclination, appear like the trees in a thick forest.'
Doshi, 'The Revelation'

an opportunity to explore all his new concepts. He is very innovative and hence it should match his needs. In technological terms, it should challenge all the usual conventions of architecture, be made of simple materials but should show how to be natural, like Kahn spoke of what the brick wanted to be.

'In short, what I want you to do is to start afresh, forget that you are an architect and design this building using your innermost sensibility. Become and be part of the process rather than an outsider.'

Kurma then continued to project the simple, yet very skilfully crafted tribal huts, the bamboo structures of the Nagas, the mud huts of Rajasthanis. I suddenly realized that even today we have the adivasis (the tribals) who lead a simple life and for them to build natural forms is as natural as breathing. What they need perhaps is guidance. Kurma was perhaps reading my thoughts and said that, 'like timeless legends which depict the aspirations of man, here is your chance to connect our ancient traditions of crafts with new technologies aided with computers.'

Lastly, Kurma talked about the site of the Gufa and the campus where had I designed one of my earliest buildings. He said that, 'Now, after almost thirty-five years, you should demonstrate all that you have experienced and learned in life, all that you now understand about architecture and your design should manifest all your recent concerns and pursuits.' At this point, I felt shaken and to my surprise, I found my

wife Kamu trying to wake me up because it was well past eight in the morning. Having experienced this dialogue and vision, I decided to again begin work on this project and set up a team following the advice of Kurma.

What you see today is the labour of love of many colleagues, and my friends to realize the vision hidden below ground. All along they have shed their prejudices and worked wholeheartedly on this concept. For example, from the mythical images, Lise drew sketches of the Gufa but it was then conceived in brick. Then Ranga Rao with Vishnu Joshi conceptualized the soap bubbles and the fruits which have their own natural stable configurations. To this Ravindra Vasavada added his experiences of Frei Otto's tensile, cantenary structures. Anilbhai Patel and Suresh Shah helped to construct this rather unusual building with masons and adivasis. They all helped to realize this strange-looking object.

But what is most fascinating now is the manner of its use and its magnetic quality which attracts all those who happen to see it. During your visit today, you must have noticed the children, wearing all kinds of colours in their dresses, who enjoy being on the white glazed domes as well as on the lush green lawns. For them, the glistening smooth surfaces of the domes are more exciting than the metal slides in the public parks. For them the reflecting, three-dimensional curves of surfaces offer a whole new tactile experience.

The protuberances on the surfaces perhaps remind you of telescopes or the bulging eyes of the chameleons, crocodiles or the frogs. As you will observe tonight, they will act as torches and their positions will so light the surrounding trees and landscape that it will appear as if it is a moonscape. I hope you have noticed the hundred and one neem trees that surround this new Gufa. They protect the place as if it is a paradise.

But what is unexpected is the experience inside. Are you not surprised to find that it is larger than you had imagined and deceptive in its forms? The skylights that you had seen on the roof as protuberances are not immediately visible, yet the light that they let in makes the Gufa space glow, lending it an almost ethereal quality. The columns, even though occurring at random and of varied thickness, some an inclination, appear like the trees in a thick forest. But if you observe them carefully, they are actually the supporting elements transferring the loads very naturally. As I said earlier, our attempt has been to make this building stress-free by transferring the gravity naturally.

Then there are the two large rotundas. They are meant for discourses on art and culture. And of course you can never miss tile walls and the free-standing sculptures. They are the real masterpieces of Husain. What he has tried here is to create a wonderful counterpoint by locating the painting at strategic surfaces so that his stories can be interpreted in many, many ways.

Before I end, I must tell you about an event that took place when the building was consecrated. The tribals who had worked to construct it were so deeply affected by the technique of construction, the form of the building and the way changes could be made naturally, that they felt they were reliving their own ancient ritual of Pithora Bava. So, what they did was to perform a dance, following a puja and the sprinkling of sacred colours. These nocturnal rituals lasted for nine days. But on the first day on hearing the chanting of Sheshnaga (Lord Vishnu's nine-hooded Cobra), Husain suddenly got up, held a large brush in his hand and climbed the domes. He feverishly painted in oil on the still-incomplete glazed domes a large cobra connecting the two large rotundas. Then he asked me to get his cobra glazed in black mosaic. No sooner was the painting of cobra complete on the ninth day than the tribals declared that prana, the breath of life from the God Pithora Bava has now entered the Gufa. Thus the Sheshnaga's coils established a contact with Kurma and precisely at that moment it rained, even though out of season.

# 10
# National Institute of Fashion Technology, *New Delhi, 1997*

The fashion industry in India is a mainstay of its rapidly expanding economy. Its increasing prominence is a natural consequence of its historical leadership in textile design and production, in which it also retains an impressive international market share. To encourage the fast-growing garment industry, the government of India decided to establish a National Institute of Fashion Technology (NIFT) in Delhi to provide education in clothing design as a service to the ready-made garment industry. New research in this field, in keeping with India's cultural heritage, and training personnel in the field of garment marketing were also important objectives of the project. The Institute was visualized as an international fashion centre and, more importantly, as a prototypical agency promoting regional institutes all over India to encourage local talent and resources, and to enrich the national garment design and manufacturing industry. It had to be easily accessible to local and foreign professionals, visitors and buyers. A centrally located site of 3.5 acres in Hauz Khas was selected, but due to encroachments and other technical difficulties, the site was constricted to 2.87 acres (11,642 square metres).

In addition to these general goals, the client specifically requested that the Institute offer several part-time morning and evening classes for employees of the trade, using people from the trade as well

**Above** Bridge above entrance with square window cut into the side wall.

**Opposite** Entrance at the top of the sunken court. The centre of the complex takes advantage of a narrow site plan to create a dramatic descent to a pool, with reflective angled glass multiplying the effect.

as academics for teaching assignments. There was also to be a foreign faculty. In addition, the client asked for a resource centre, consisting of a library, an Indian and Western garment and textile collection, a research laboratory and design studios, not only to be used by the industry, but as an example to the

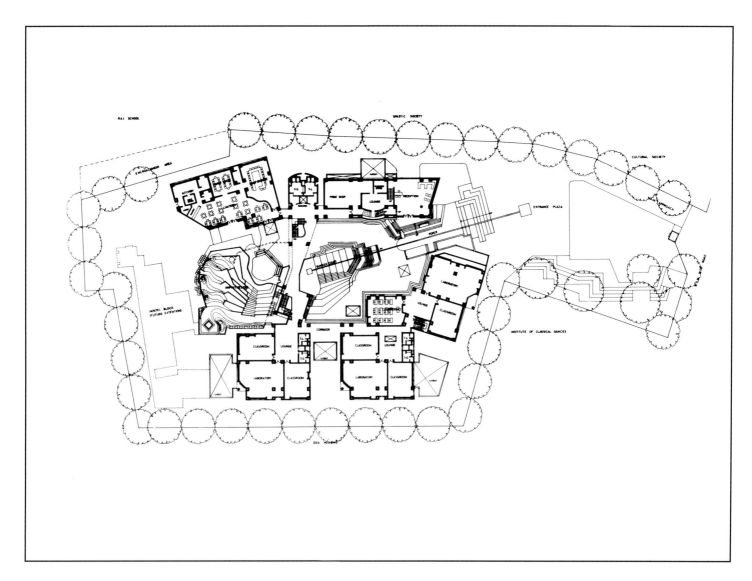

**Above** Plan, ground floor. Regular office buildings are wedded to the irregular shape of the site by enhancing uneven natural features in the inner court, which descends in a series of steps (at the centre of the plan). To the left is an amphitheatre.

**Right** The site is surrounded by housing and institutional buildings.

**Opposite** Plan, basement level. An auditorium occupies the space directly beneath the amphitheatre (at the left of the plan). The rest of the basement is used for car parking spaces and mechanical facilities.

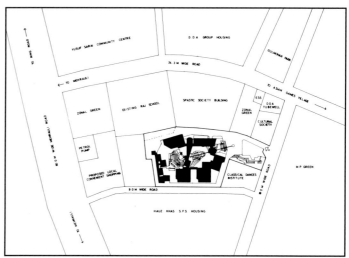

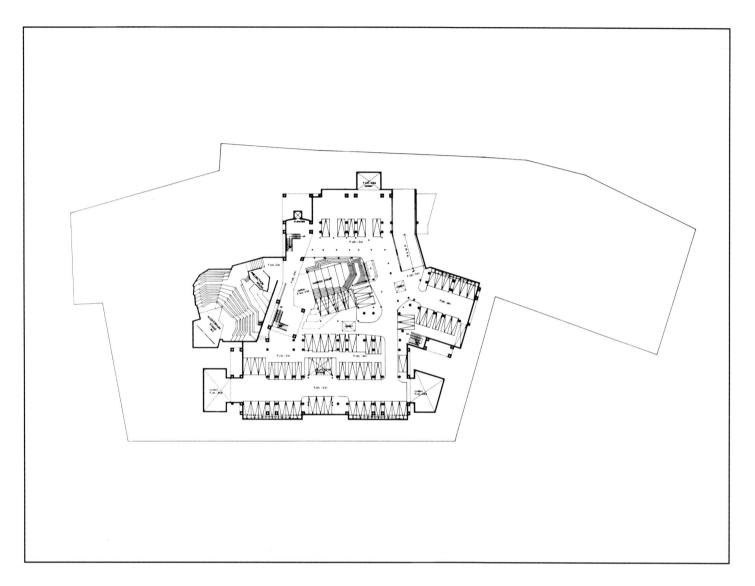

general public, as well as exporters' showrooms, textile manufacturers' showrooms and outlets for the sale of Indian fashion goods.

The site is located just off the Mehrauli road with an approach from a road leading to Asian Games Village. Access is through a plot set aside as green space now given over to NIFT on condition that no building be built on this part of the land, which was calculated in Floor Area Ratio (FAR) considerations. The NIFT site is surrounded by housing and institutional uses. Fortunately, only one institutional building for the Spastic Society designed by architect Romi Khosla, occupies part of the north side of the NIFT property.

The other two plots are reserved for a cultural society and a classical dance institute.

While allocating the plot, the Delhi Development Authority (DDA) stipulated certain conditions: that the permissible FAR will not exceed one hundred so that NIFT can only build on an area equivalent to the site allocated; that the maximum ground coverage will not exceed 25 per cent of the total site area; that a basement up to 50 per cent of the total area is permissible but may not extend beyond the set back lines, and that this basement can be used only for car parking and mechanical facilities; any other use of the basement will be calculated in the FAR but not in the ground cover.

**Above and right** A glazed walkway of reflective glass looks down into the sunken court.

**Opposite** The protruding edges of the square window, cut away to reveal the bridge above the entrance which links the administration block to the academic block. The steps down to the water recall the magnificent step wells near Ahmedabad.

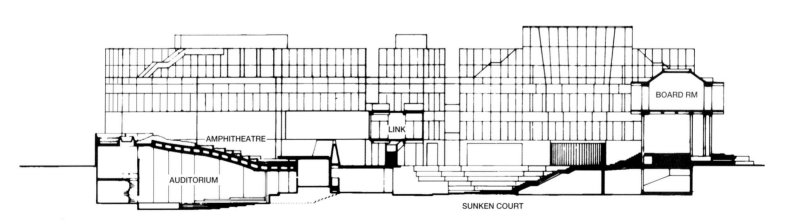

AUDITORIUM    AMPHITHEATRE    LINK    BOARD RM    SUNKEN COURT

They also stipulated that the maximum height of the building from the ground should not exceed 15 metres; otherwise it would be classified as multi-storeyed building and would have to fulfil many additional bylaws applicable to a 'fire-hazardous building'. Lastly, they required that the green plot provided for access should be suitably landscaped and be free of any construction. Though car parking at 1.14 car spaces per 92.93 square metres of built-up area is required to be provided in the basement, the DDA agreed that the Institute have 50 per cent of total parking requirement provided in the basement and the remainder on the ground surface.

Given the ambitious objectives specified by the client, as well as the strict DDA bylaws, Doshi arrived at the following conclusion:

Fashion design demands continuous innovation. For this changing environment, highly visible display and show areas are essential Fashion shows are indeed theatrical acts with an emphasis on dramatic effects. All this implies continuous movement in space and time which must be modulated. In architectural terms, this suggests an introverted bazaar-like atmosphere enlivened by the movement of the students and the visitors. The theatrical element suggests a series of

**Opposite** Glazed walkway overlooking the sunken court.

**Above** The same facade, seen through open walkways.

Views from above the sunken court.

**Above** Central water channel leading from outside into the heart of the complex. The bridge spans the area above it, linking the two main buildings. The entrance to the court is at the top of the steps to the left below the bridge.

**Left** Angled glazed surfaces of the administration block.

**Opposite** Section showing the two blocks joined by the bridge. The upper floors of the administration block on the left overhang the lower floors, as in the architecture of traditional *havelis* (mansions).

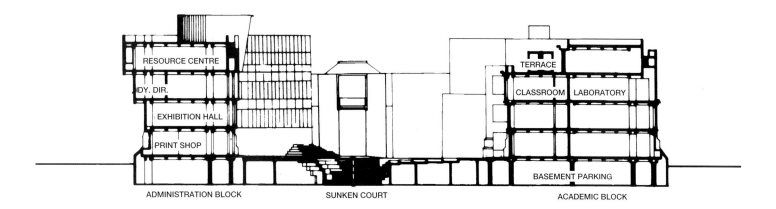

RESOURCE CENTRE
DY. DIR.
EXHIBITION HALL
PRINT SHOP
TERRACE
CLASSROOM  LABORATORY
BASEMENT PARKING
ADMINISTRATION BLOCK          SUNKEN COURT          ACADEMIC BLOCK

high and low platforms, a variety of galleries, and areas for formal and casual activities and direct and indirect display of the designs. This implies a series of internal courtyards and terraces at various heights.

To achieve this introspective image, the front court, stipulated by the DDA as a green area for access, only became a bazaar with opportunities for display, social gatherings and public or semi-public activities. The administrative block, located in the foreground of the complex with library and exhibition area, is more formal than the classroom clusters beyond, which are grouped together to form units of classrooms, laboratories, and service spaces with a common lobby. The clusters connect to the main administrative building with a bridge overlooking the two active courtyards, which also serves to separate them visually. In addition, behind the classroom clusters there are dormitories and a rector's suite along with the guest-rooms which create a domestic scale of their own. Part of the common rooms and the rector's apartment overlook the courtyards and the major access linking the courtyards, as well as the main entrance court, with its cascading fountains.

The exterior of the complex is related to the surrounding buildings. It respects the Spastic Institute by opening up to it at an appropriate level, as well as to the housing. The Institute has an undulating painted steel pergola above the internal courts as a symbolic gateway to be seen by visitors across the park as they make their way toward the entrance, where the Institute hangs fabrics produced by its students during their fashion shows or occasions such as convocation.

The gate announces the activities of the Institute in the form of artifacts and costumes all year round, with its flight of steps leading to two courtyards. The first is in the form of a modified *kund*, or saucer-shaped rainwater store, and the other is an informal amphitheatre. Both form the central space of the Institute and have glazed corridors around them that allow a clear view of the galleries, the classroom clusters, the administration block, and library and the dormitory blocks.

Doshi's concept of surrounding the court with each of the main blocks of the complex of buildings between three and four storeys high rather than one monolithic, massive building block, gives the ensemble a less institutional aspect and was intended to replicate the feeling of a traditional *chowk* (courtyard) or *moholla* (market square) and to foster a sense of a community. The variety of functions in each building were intended to allow each to acquire its own character, making each identifiable within a unified vocabulary.

Step well at Adalaj, near Ahmedabad, 1502. This monument once served as a Hindu sanctuary, as well as a water source. Many features reappear at Doshi's National Institute of Fashion Technology (NIFT).

**Left and below** A wealth of ornate carving decorates the surfaces. At the NIFT, reflective glass gives a comparable 'dematerialized' surface effect. Columns, beams and steps create dramatic perspectives downwards to the water source.

**Opposite** Walkways look out through wide openings.

# Architect's Story

In order to build an architectural complex unique for the institute, a concept was conceived around a story. This fictional narration may help understand the intents of the architecture.

Long ago where the present NIFT campus is built, there was a small village built of mud walls painted white. This settlement though small, was very beautiful. There were many cattle, few trees and a central place. In this central place there was a small pond surrounded by steps. This small waterbody was a very sacred place, perhaps due to the scarcity of water. When asked, the villagers said that they had to dig deep to get this water which they found only at this spot.

Because of this great effort required and the fear that the water may eventually disappear, the villagers made this spot a place of pilgrimage. Several times in a year, many other persons from the surrounding villages gathered to meet, sing and even select their future companions. To perform the rituals, they built steps out of bricks and these steps took the shape of an irregular hill with several platforms. Perhaps these platforms helped the different groups to use them for simultaneous activities.

After few decades, the sanctity of the place raised the importance of this place. As a result other rather well-to-do persons built few houses in this area in wood and stone. These houses had beautiful jharokhas, balconies, jalis, verandahs and several blank walls carved with the events of their daily life. With growing population and changing economic conditions, the houses and the activities started expanding. As a result, a few rich persons built some haveli-like structures in other empty spots. However, all this building activity respected the central sacred water body. The rich people, in order to propitiate the gods and due to their concern for the community welfare, built low walls around the steps, improved the finishes of the steps. Continuously growing popularity of the sacred place required facilities for the pilgrims so a small ashram-like place was built with rooms for pilgrims.

During the last century many upgradations and renovations of the building took place. However, to retain the sense of belonging to the past, a few areas of the building were kept intact. Any new material or treatment that was added to the building became like a collage. New large windows were juxtaposed with the small carved windows of the older buildings.

Over the years, the village was totally engulfed by large developments and it became a minuscule part of the new urban scene of the twentieth century. The new laws of hygiene were introduced. Water supply and drainage were provided. For this upgradation the buildings were cut in many parts. As a result the building became fragments of earlier continuous complex.

However, with increasing demand on this land and fast social and cultural changes, many of the early inhabitants sold their properties. They moved away with the fortunes to live their own life because the place was gradually *acquiring altogether a different meaning — very different from the quiet life of the earlier days.*

*Whereas in the recent past, as one gathers, many corporate bodies, desirous of acquiring spiritual support from this sacred place, purchased some of the properties and changed them internally to accommodate their contemporary needs. These corporate bodies were then thriving in their enterprise, thanks to the holy atmosphere!*

*But to preserve the sanctity of this place from adverse changes, the archaeological authorities have decided to acquire this property and pass it on to an Institute which could not only simulate the old life but also add a new present-day dimension to it. The authorities believe that this is the only place where we could trace a history of many centuries.*

*Luckily the National Institute of Fashion Technology has found this complex near Hauz-Khas where the Institute will not only retain the unique character of this place but also provide sufficient impetus through certain modifications so that the history of our times will become a link to the past.*

Plan of the Adalaj step well, near Ahmedabad. The long flight of steps descends to an octagonal well through a dramatic series of columns.

# BHARAT DIAMOND BOURSE

**Below and right** Preliminary sketches, Bharat Diamond Bourse.

**Opposite** Models of a single unit (**above**) and the whole complex (**below**).

# 11
# Bharat Diamond Bourse, *Mumbai, 1998*

The Bharat Diamond Bourse is Doshi's largest project to date, a city within a city of approximately 3 million square feet, accommodating an estimated 30,000 people on a 20-acre site. The Bourse project is intended to bring all of the activities of the diamond trade together in one place. The diamond industry is one of the fastest growing in India and, due to impending liberalization of economic policies regarding exports, it promises to become even more prominent. The new Bourse will strengthen the industry's global connections with other diamond centres in Tel Aviv, Antwerp, London and Los Angeles. Poor infrastructure, overcrowding and a general lack of amenities led to the commissioning of a new bourse on 17 March 1991. The original client brief consisted of offices and three trading halls following the pattern of other bourses. After visits to Tel Aviv, Antwerp and London, the architect made modifications to this brief to incorporate an emphasis on the social and cultural singularity of the urban setting and to make the project a prototype for developments of a similar scale throughout India. As finally agreed, the programme includes about 2,000 offices of various sizes for each of the members of the bourse, along with a business centre, two trading halls, conference halls, an exhibition space, three restaurants and eight cafeterias. Custom-bonded vaults and store rooms, as well as

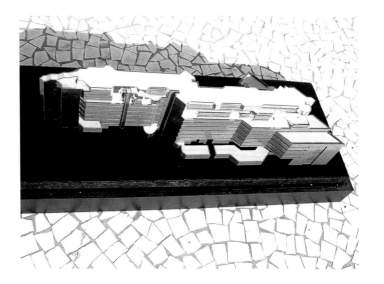

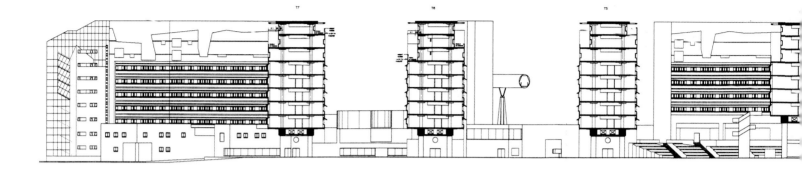

export councils, banks, a technical laboratory, courier services, post office and a telephone exchange have also been provided along with a medical and dental clinic for employees.

Of the 3 million square feet of built-up area in the Bourse, the majority are occupied by offices. The self-sufficient nature of the project is underscored by the recycling of waste water for irrigation, as well as for cooling in the air-conditioning system. The autonomous character of the architecture is driven by the paramount need for security in this mini-city. The site for the Bourse is 12 kilometres from the existing Panchratna market, more easily served by Santacruz airport, 5 kilometres away, and the Bandra railway station, 3 kilometres away. The site is trapezoidal, with the longest sides facing north and south. Climatic analysis showed that the prevailing summer wind comes from the southwest corner of the site, while the winter wind comes from the southeast. Mumbai's climate is characterized by intense heat and humidity with maximum and minimum temperatures in summer ranging from 32 to 28 degrees centigrade, only falling to 26 to 19 degrees in the winter. In response to these severe environmental conditions, as well as to the high water table on the site's reclaimed land which had rocky strata only a few metres below the surface, Doshi attempted to position the buildings for minimum solar

exposure, while still allowing as much natural light as possible into the spaces where the diamonds are sorted. He also oriented the blocks towards the prevailing winds, as well as to create courtyards that could be used by occupants of the Bourse during leisure time.

It was Doshi's primary intention that the complex present a viable environmental alternative to the corporate megastructures now becoming ubiquitous throughout Asia. The design strategy that Doshi adopted to achieve this had six parts. His first and most obvious tactic has been the distribution of functions in twelve lightning-bolt-shaped low-rise bar buildings rather than a single tower. Secondly, these rise out of a uniform field of common facilities organized around courtyards and shaded 'streets' at ground level (the courtyard is a well proven device for climatic control in this region). Thirdly, the slim bars, served by double-loaded corridors, are strategically positioned to create 'wind tunnels' that guide the prevailing winds toward the project through a large green park on the eastern edge, which the main trading hall and a majority of public amenities face. The disadvantage of this more dispersed urban model has been that security has had to be broken down into ten individual checkpoints, rather than being centralized, as it would be in a tower, with five security points for members. This may actually be argued to be an advantage, since each member of the

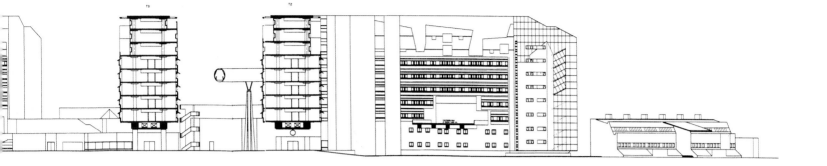

Site sections. By building twelve low-rise buildings instead of a giant single high-rise, favoured for so many modern city offices, Doshi provides courtyards and shaded 'streets' – not only for natural climatic control, but also for access to common public amenities.

Bourse has greater control of its own operations and the separate sections devoted to each of the members are discrete units with their own personality.

A fourth strategy was the use of local rather than imported resources, a mainstay of the sustainable philosophy. In selecting materials the guiding principles were durability, weathering characteristics and minimum maintenance. During the 1980s, many new building materials and processes became available in India and the Vastu-Shilpa Foundation is monitoring the long-term behaviour of materials in the face of the heavy pollution, monsoons and humidity of Mumbai, which have historically been the enemies of industrially produced products. Doshi's experience with the deterioration of exposed reinforced concrete in the early part of his career, as seen in the Institute of Indology and the School of Architecture in Ahmedabad, has lent a certain degree of urgency and mission to this issue. His latest buildings, such as the Gufa, may be grouped along with this much more focused effort to find a viable alternative that performs well in a severe set of circumstances. This is one of the most significant, but least recognized, items on the agenda of Doshi's latest work: making the wrapper adaptable to the severe environmental conditions in the various regions of India where he has built and is building.

Site sections. By building twelve low-rise buildings instead of a giant single high-rise, favoured for so many modern city offices, Doshi provides courtyards and shaded 'streets' – not only for natural climatic control, but also for access to common public amenities.

In addition to low-rise clustering, Doshi has favoured internal courtyards, orientation to promote natural ventilation, and the selection of indigenous telluric, rather than imported, industrial materials with far higher embodied energy. A fifth sustainable principle in the project is self-sufficiency. Already alluded to in the recycling of waste water, this attitude is more generally manifest in Doshi's approach to this huge complex as 'a string of pearls', or a unit that is perfected and then replicated. This not only allows each of the member zones to be more humanly scaled, but also contributes to the overall efficiency of the entire complex, by reducing energy use. No matter how effective natural ventilation is, air-conditioning is considered necessary in this instance to bring the Bourse up to expected corporate standards, especially since offices in each zone are rented and must be commercially competitive and viable.

In spite of such rational standardization, Doshi has never lost sight of the sixth and most important sustainable issue of all: retaining or improving quality of life within an environmentally conscious framework.

# BHARAT DIAMOND BOURSE

Details of architect's model of the Bourse. Open spaces and angles of light and shade are key planning considerations. Each part of the building is designed to present as little facade as possible to the sun, and to exploit the prevailing breeze to full advantage.

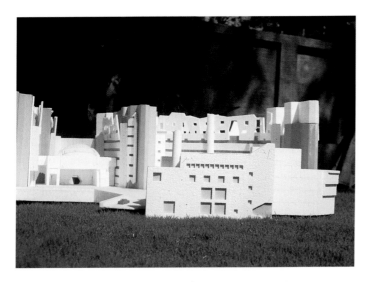

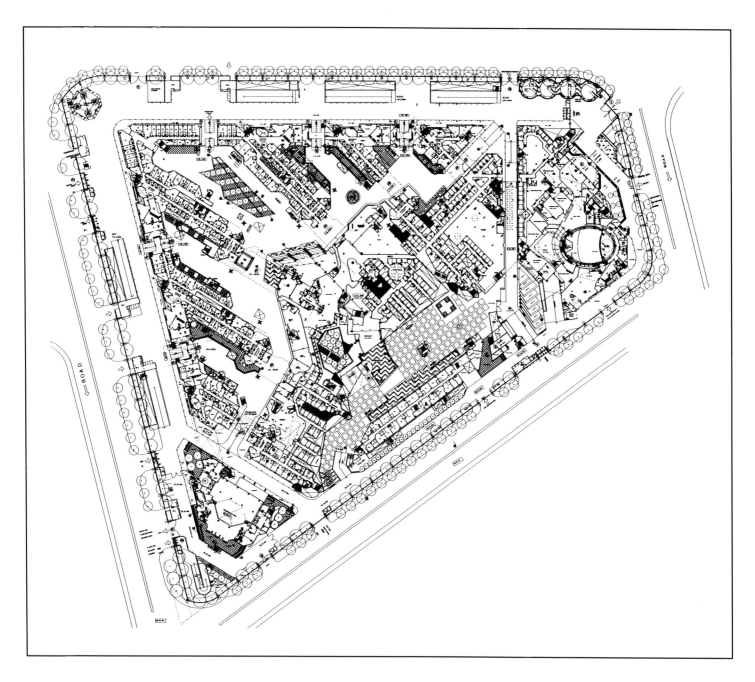

**Above** Site plan. The buildings are placed together in such a way
as to funnel wind between the blocks.

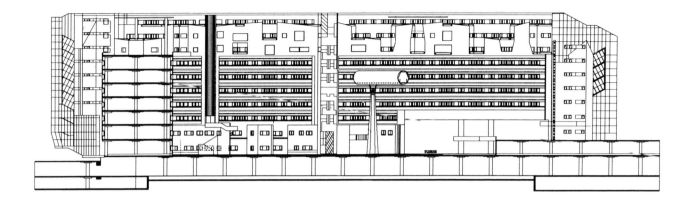

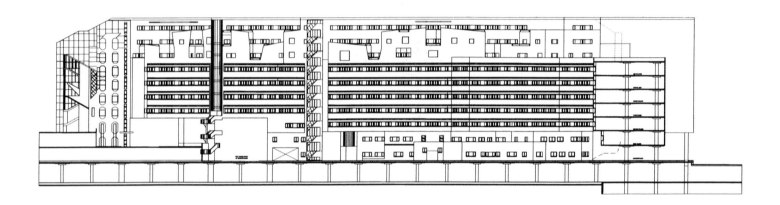

He has done this by focusing on images, as his 'story' at the end of this discussion suggests, of translating the natural essence of Mumbai into a synthesis of built and landscaped form. These images include the sea and perfumed sea breezes, the port and the terraces cut into the Malabar hills, in the local context; there are broader references to the philosophical notion of 'blurring the edge', the comparison of the finite and infinite found in the *Gopurams*, that historically has made the Indian approach to the tower so different. Reflective glass has been used on various parts of the linear blocks, especially near the corners, to assist in this 'dematerialization', with surfaces as high as 80 metres, mirroring the block across the way and the courts and gardens in between. This continues the metaphor of the crystalline, diamond-encrusted cave that was central to the architect's initial design vision, but also provides a more topical related reference to the importance of the film industry in Mumbai, which creates an ineffable magical realm of its own.

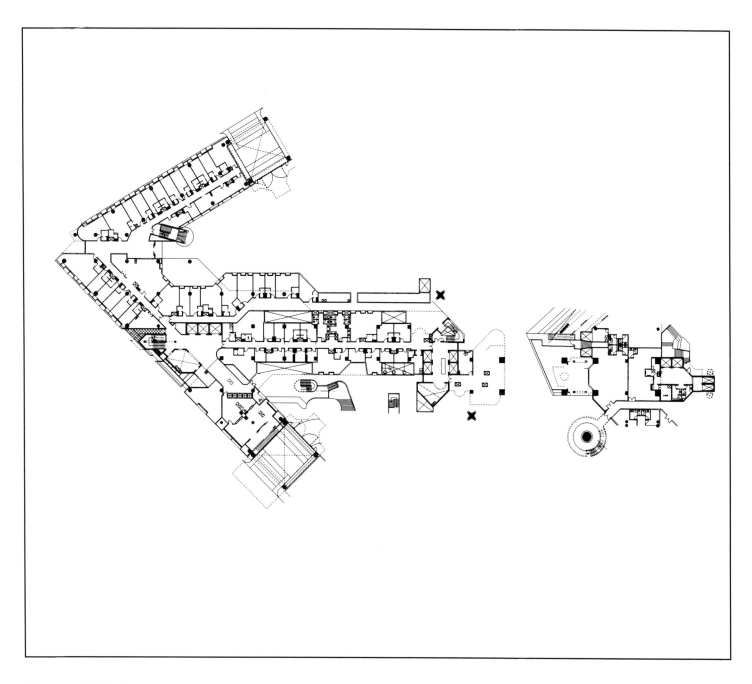

**Above** Detail of plan shows the funnel effect.

**Opposite** Tower 4, elevations from two sides of the building. On the facade
of the upper parts of the building, protective 'wrapping' is a characteristic
means of controlling temperature

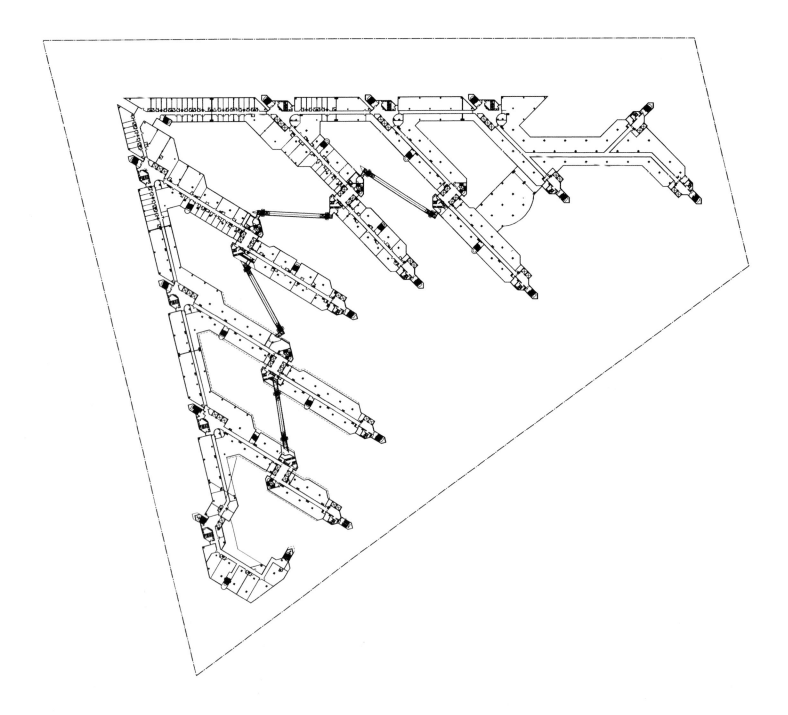

# Legend of the Living Rock

In my entire career as an architect I have never experienced a phenomenon such as the one that happened on the night of June 17, 1992 and which controlled my destiny for more than four years till August 26, 1996, to be precise.

It began with our appointment as architects for designing the Bharat Diamond Bourse at Bandra. After signing the contract, we visited the site. During our visit, we discussed with the clients their image of this bourse and the only description they kept repeating was that it should be unique. Perhaps they meant that like a diamond, this bourse should sparkle with its exclusiveness. We also discussed the approach to the site as well as the nature of building, its location and phasing of the construction to meet an extremely tight schedule for such a large project.

Following these discussions a conceptual design was prepared. After this was approved, we prepared a final design and the execution drawings to commence the foundation of the diaphragm wall and a portion of the basement. All the drawings for this work were prepared at breakneck speed. The building contractor procured the latest machinery at site and started excavating the site to reach the bed rock at a depth of about 10 metres.

Then on the night of June 17, a date I will never forget, we received an urgent call from the building contractor. He asked us to reach the site at the earliest and could not explain the alarming urgency except constantly to express awe and wonder about something at the site and even sounded frightened.

All of us reached there within a few hours and what we saw at the site is even today unbelievable. The location and forms of the buildings, the peculiar spaces and the materials that you now see and experience in the new Bourse have been powerfully shaped by what we witnessed on that night. I do not know about others who were present but at least I would call it the greatest miracle in my life.

We saw the site excavated to a depth of about 10 metres and the bed rock which now lay exposed appeared like a giant crystal on that dark night. I had never before seen the patterns and textures which I saw on this 350 metre long and 250 metre wide rock.

Apart from these, two features made this rock unique. Almost in the centre of this rather flat 8-hectare rock, there was a glowing outcrop, like a stub. It was rather large for its height but in its transparency and formation, it had the character of a beautiful, uncut diamond. It appeared that its glow was generated from its efforts to pull the whole land mass up, almost like the mythological story of churning of the sea, samudra manthan. On close observations, we found that this central stub was indeed pulling the 8-hectare rock up, slowly yet surely. It was an astounding experience like the eruption of lava from Mount Etna which I had witnessed.

Because of this unusual phenomenon we had no recourse but to immediately summon all the scientists, scholars and pundits we knew to the site. After studying this phenomenon each one had his story to tell. However, one elderly pundit casually wondered if this site perhaps could be the lost fragment of land and jewel which emerged during the samudra manthan *when the great jewel with Goddess Daxmi appeared on the earth. We asked the scientists from Tata Institute of Fundamental Research, Atomic Energy Commission and other national laboratories to tell us what should we do so that we could continue the construction.*

*We took extensive photographs of this moving land mass from several angles so that we could unravel the hidden meanings behind the peculiarities of this whole phenomenon. We then began to rethink our project with the help of the photographs and the hidden messages that the site conveyed. Being a religious person, I took this event as a God-sent opportunity to integrate the complex to the site.*

*On overlaying the enlarged photographs on our final design drawings, it became clear to us that this site must be an ancient quarry from where the last* ratna *(jewel) emerged. We also felt that this quarry must have been a major trading centre of precious stones in the ancient past. These thoughts came to most of us from observations of the features on the site. We wondered as to how there were 20-metre-wide levelled surfaces along the periphery like roads for transporting the goods? How come there were ramp-like slopes going up and down? Were they, perhaps, connecting different levels for vehicles which were either parked or moved for loading operations?*

*Apart from this peripheral road-like strip, there was another sunken strip, very straight, like our present day service roads* leading to parking. Strangely, the spacing between the first strip and this one was almost the same as what we had provided in our plans. The distance between those strips was exactly the same as that we used for doubly loaded parking.

*We also noticed large chunks of (almost two storeys high) blocks located at a different level. The blocks were oriented southwest and open spaces between these were again of the same size that we find in our ancient towns. It seemed like we were either seeing a model of the city at Mohenjo daro or an electronic circuit because the orientation of most of these blocks was precisely the same.*

*We wondered whether this discipline in orientation was suggestive of any value. Perhaps this was a hint for us to plan the offices for natural breeze and also to protect major areas from incident radiation. Next to these two-storeyed, nearly 40-metre-wide blocks there was yet another, rather irregular strip encircling the last stretch of two-storeyed land mass. The surface of this stretch had slight undulations and was punctured with holes of about 3 metres diameter, as if to allow light and ventilation to a lower level of the quarry. Perhaps the lower level was also used for purposes like our proposal of using a basement for parking and other services.*

*But what fascinated all of us the most was the central stub. It was relatively small but very powerful like a grip that could pull the total rock. Its location, glow and form appeared to attract all the three strips of say streets. Surrounding this hub, if we can call it so, lay several fissures. They were all running* in the southwest direction except that they converged near the edge in the form of a slab at an angle. Its angle reminded us of the amphitheatres that we usually provide in a small town for gathering. The area between the amphitheatre and the hub had shallow but distinct levels, as if to allow people to gather and celebrate life or to attend special functions located near this powerful column. It was like a great pivot.

Beyond this space there was another large area which was rather flat. It had no distinct character except its location in the northeast corner. This is, incidentally, the most auspicious place for entrances prescribed in our ancient treatises and I was pleasantly surprised to note that this is the same location from where our scheme had provided the main entrance.

Having discovered these clues from the living rock mass, we came to believe that there is a hidden reason for the diamond bourse to be located on this site. Rather than worrying over this unusual phenomenon we accepted this situation with grace and decided to integrate our buildings with this land mass in an appropriate manner. Along with the clients, we consulted the scientists, technocrats and pundits to find ways and means to somehow freeze this land mass in its position to suit our basement, ground and upper-level proposals. This way our parking, services and the peripheral accesses to the site could become part of the ancient land mass and our upper levels could be suitably adjusted to the higher land formations.

In order to realize this God-sent gift to the fullest potential, we summoned the best technologists in the world.

Finally we contacted the agency which had with great faith, devotion and skill worked on the relocation of the Abu Simbel temple in Egypt. With their help we managed to freeze this land mass such that the bourse complex acquires unique character, the base in the form of the undulating terraced earth and the towers as our additions.

What you see here at the bourse at the main entrance is the original rock and the central crystal shaped building; the trading hall, that you notice in the second larger court is our addition to the original stub which we now call our ratna (jewel). The amphitheatre to the west of this hall is the original slope partially modified by us. We have added underneath it all the public facilities for visitors. The 6-metre-high wall encircling this main space is the original quarry wall. We have punctured it to provide some light and ventilation to some of our offices which we have located in its thickness.

The fissures emanating from the stub or the central pillar of the trading hall have been slightly changed. Some are widened to create several interlinked water pools where you also see fountains of various sizes and shapes. These fountains have now become a part of our festivals. During summer they help to keep the area cool.

As you know, this bourse is now a major tourist attraction. Beyond this point admissions are restricted only to members of our bourse. However, the visitors are not totally cut off from the rest of the complex. Over the 6-metre-high wall one can see lots of plantation as well as people strolling. They are our bourse members who meet their colleagues on this promenade. Along this route are located facilities such as bourse offices, banks, stores, restaurants, etc. This rampart-like terrace also overlooks the other green area and the trees planted by us. You can also see the terraces of smaller office blocks where terraced gardens have appeared. These trees and shrubs in the green area again are another wonder. These were not planted by us but grew out of the seeds that were lying dormant in the crevices for centuries. If you go close, you will notice that their colours, textures and formations are very different from the ones you find in this region.

During monsoon, with torrential rains, these crevices become water channels. The rainwater from the terraces converges at the main thick wall that you see from here. It flows out of the gargoyles that you see in cascades. These cascades remind one of the Italian gardens, particularly the garden of Este. In other seasons during festivals and on holidays, we create these cascades by recycling water from fountains on the terraces.

You must have by now noticed that there are three major elements that dominate the form of the bourse. First, the granite base and the 6-metre-high stone wall, second, the water channels and the fountains, and third, the green valleys formed on the lower terraces. All this is our homage to the moving land mass which we froze to remind us of the sites of our ancient cities like Babylon or Mohenjo daro where love for earth, water, sky, light and air was paramount.

You must be, I am sure, by now anxious to ask me about the towers that rise above this ancient base. Yes, they were added by us to create space for our members' offices. They are our high-tech additions in contemporary style. The north face of the towers is covered with mirrored curtain wall to create a fragile and transparent environment. But if you go up you will notice that all the alternate panels sparkle and reflect the sun rays, like a diamond's facades that sparkle with light. These diamond shaped pyramids are provided in each office glass panel to give the merchants a multi-dimensional view of Bombay's skyline. This way their visions are broadened and they also provide them relief from constantly watching diamonds through magnifying lenses.

On the southern side of these towers, we have small windows to protect the offices from direct sun. However to give them a sense of wide expanses, we have provided projections with coloured mirror glass over the windows so that the view of the sky is softer and when seen from the lower level, they can observe the lush green terraces or trees planted around and within the site. With such a sacred ancient rock by way of site, you must be wondering how we were able to construct such large crystal-shaped tower slabs. Well, we have tried to minimize the supporting structure of these towers and we have established their angles and locations on the basis of punctures which existed in the ancient rock.

There are altogether nine towers and as you may notice, we have provided bridges on alternate floors to interlink them.

These are clad in mirrored glass and depending upon the sky and sun conditions they may be visible and sometimes not. Viewed from here, you can only see two bridges but there are actually five of them.

We felt that the 'living' base can only be complemented without disturbing its tortoise like character if our towers were thin, oriented towards north-south and had no regular shape. With minimum supports they also give an impression of hovering in the sky.

Lastly, I want to show you the jewel of our bourse, the trading hall located on the third floor which is almost floating. It has the most magnificent interior. Its ceiling is made of shining metal sheets punctured at selected spots to allow glimpses of the sky, the sun and the stars. But, its orientation and cover, made of special lenses, cut out the glare during the day and offer a clear view of the stars at night. The structure of the ceiling is totally concealed to make the roof of the trading hall a part of the sky. We feel that this way, the merchants will experience greater freedom.

The walls and the floors of the trading hall are a combination of hard and soft, shiny and dull surfaces. This way the space looks relaxed, a vital need for the diamond merchants constantly operating under stress. The original stub at the ground level is now part of our central focus. It is related to the diamond museum and its reflecting surfaces are a part of our daily tourist attraction.

Even though there are many things that I can show you and talk about, the time is short and perhaps you may call me again, but before we part, I want to narrate to you something which may interest you and you may like to ponder over.

This place, because of the ancient rock which has been made a part of our design, has now become the most sacred place in India. All those who come here feel elated and as we have heard from many, their life becomes peaceful and also successful. Here there is constant breeze and we experience the sea. Here the fountains, the walls and the gardens make people forget the Hanging Gardens. Here the sky seems bluer and cleaner than it perhaps is because here silence can be heard. This place has now become a true sanctuary.

# Conclusion

Balkrishna Doshi has a much larger following in India than he does internationally, despite the fact that he has realized over one hundred large-scale projects over his long career. There is no denying that he is something of a cult figure among certain architects around the world, primarily because of his concerted attempt to establish a truly appropriate contemporary vocabulary of built form for his country, but generally his work is not widely known. Because of the extent of his commitment, he can be considered along with surprisingly few others, past and present, who have attempted to do the same thing for their own countries or extended identities and have achieved the same degree of relative global anonymity for their efforts: Hassan Fathy, Sedad Hakki Elden, Abdel Wahed el-Wakil, Rasem Badran, Geoffrey Bawa and Jimmy Lim among a handful of others.

What links all of these diverse talents is a firm grounding in Modernist dogma, delivered through a variety of conduits in their own countries or abroad. Doshi's exposure to this was more direct than the formal education in architecture received by many of the others. His four years as an apprentice in the Paris office of Le Corbusier, largely spent working on the High Court Building in Chandigarh, was a more pronounced influence than others have had, with the exception of Rasem Badran's training for the same length of time at the Hochschule Baukunst in Stuttgart in the early 1970s. As a young man, Doshi eagerly sought to understand and learn from the West. Local mythology about him includes a well known story about his appetite for knowledge and long hours spent in the library of the Architectural Association in London. What sets him apart from others of his generation is his dedication to understand what he realized he could not change and to understand it quickly.

The story that remains untold is how he changed the direction of the history of modern architecture through this passion and through the unparalleled opportunity to interact with two of its most important theorists and practitioners. He is often viewed, mistakenly, as having been in a mentor-apprentice relationship with both Le Corbusier and Louis Kahn and, while he still refers to the builder of Chandigarh as 'my guru', the mythology about Doshi also extends to his penchant for speaking his mind and his tendency to respond to the Swiss master whenever possible. Who knows the extent to which such responses and his involvement as the project manager on the High Court Building resulted in its becoming the most environmentally and contextually responsive and culturally sensitive of all the monumental, official buildings in the new city? Compared to the thin profile and orientation of the Secretariat, in which the longest sides of its linear form receive the longest exposure to the sun and make it a case study in how *not* to build in a tropical climate, or a temperate one for that matter, the High Court is a paragon of climatic propriety. The high parasol roof projected above a flatter roof is one of the first instances of a major formal recognition of regional environmental conditions to be found during this last phase of the pioneering period of the Modern movement, a profile that is frequently glossed over as being no more than a metaphor. The high, partially detached roof in fact not only serves as an umbrella to shade the second roof below, but is also shaped to act as a wind tunnel to accelerate the high breeze and draw it through the funnels between the roofs, cooling the flat surface below by natural ventilation. Much attention has been paid to the use of admixtures in the concrete of the High Court, which echoes the saffron reds and marigold yellows used in turbans and saris, but this more significant separation has received scant commentary in the past, especially its likely influence on the American Embassy at Luanda, Angola, designed by Louis Kahn ten years later.

Kahn used this opportunity in a similar climate to refine the High Court concept of a double roof by making the top segment flat, as a frame for U-shaped metal bars that covered it. Rather than just absorbing the heat, as the Corbusian parasol does, Kahn's roof acts like an automobile radiator, dissipating the heat as quickly as the bars absorb it, preventing it from reaching the flat surface below by projecting the bars on thin metal stems. Luanda was also designed to make maximum use of the prevailing wind by flanking a high open central space, also covered by the metallic screen, with two rectilinear office wings of equal size. Doshi's Institute of Indology, which has a similar *parti* without the expensive hardware due to a lower budget, predates Kahn's refinements and adds one of his own, with a garden in front and paved court behind the rectangular perimeter that accelerates the transfer of cool air through the building by convection.

All of this may seem insignificant until compared with the general progress of international-style Modernism. None of the modern icons of the late 1950s and early 1960s – Mies van der Rohe's Seagram Building and Gordon Bunshaft's Lever House for Skidmore Owings Merrill in New York in 1956, and Oscar Niemeyer's Brasilia – give any indication of climatic response. The burden is placed entirely on mechanical systems to solve temperature fluctuations. The roof was not the only double layer on Kahn's Luanda Embassy. This was also one of the earliest instances of what he called 'wrapping ruins around buildings' to modulate light and cut down on the harshness of glare in a tropical climate. Doshi wraps 'ruins' of his own around houses in Baroda at about the same time. Doshi's wall-court-house-court-wall sequence, mostly covered by a roof very much like the Luanda elevation when seen from the ends of the units, was designed for the same reasons. It is hard, if not impossible, to say who influenced whom in such cases, but Kahn's long discussion about Doshi with the students in his Master's Class at the University of Pennsylvania during the late 1960s and his obvious respect for 'this wonderful architect from India', when layered over such similarities, make it difficult to determine.

Kahn's Dacca Assembly Building, which is arguably considered his finest work, would not have been the same without his thorough knowledge of the High Court Building and Doshi's concerns about climate, addressed in the many projects that precede it. If the Indian Institute of Management at Bangalore is Doshi's 'critique' of Kahn's project at Ahmedabad, Dacca is Kahn's critique of Le Corbusier and both were intended to be objective as well as creative commentaries.

Kahn's critique extended from a knowledge about how politics are really accomplished in this and every other part of the world, in the corridors of power rather than the formal assembly rooms, to the way that an imported material like concrete is actually used in India and Pakistan. In poor countries in particular, a single band of expensive material such as marble, used to mark the break between pours of concrete, can have great psychological impact. Kahn was sensitive to people's needs. Doshi is, too, and each has marked a change in the course of Modernism.

The common explanation given for Doshi's personal intellectual growth has been that he has moved from international-style Modernism, from the sway of Le Corbusier and Louis Kahn, toward a mystical understanding of the many alien influences that have shaped the rich vernacular of his country to create a new architecture rooted in the past, which is contemporary, but not Modernist.

Rather than fitting this teleological profile, it is more likely, given the consistency of several key factors in his entire *oeuvre*, that Doshi began at variance with modern tendencies in his sensitivity to people and the environment, but otherwise has progressed in a cyclical way, refining basic principles at each level to conform to new insights about his own culture. It is useful to keep in mind Doshi's conformance to and reinvention of the following basic Modernist premises. These do not follow exactly Doshi's eight principles described earlier.

INSTITUTIONS Doshi's belief is that even the single home is an institution, the repository of the family. The extended family is still an integral part of the Indian social structure; the social fragmentation found in the West, frequently blamed on the affluence provided by industrialization, has yet to occur. Religion, too, is still an important part of Indian life, compared to the drift away from spirituality identifiable in Europe and the United States. So it is no surprise that Doshi's inspiration for the creation of institutions begins with the interaction he has witnessed when visiting a temple, moving him to recreate

> the pauses, transitional spaces and thresholds which act as catalytic agents for the built-form and the individual or the community to enter into a dialogue at the level of comprehension and this dialogue gives direction to the community at large. Built forms which generate such holistic experiences finally become human institutions.[16]

There is a sad paradox in the fact that the very institutions that Doshi is fostering, especially the management institutes he has designed, may help to accelerate the disintegration of the community, by promoting the same scenario of industrialization that has now been played out in the West.

SPACE The concern for the volume contained within a building is an undeniable legacy of the Modern movement, with structural expression, light, progression and procession, honesty of materials, and form following function all subservient to this idea. Yet the most profound shift Doshi has made, while still retaining the premise, is in the nature of space in his buildings and projects. Doshi refers to the 'mythical sense' of space in traditional architecture which he has been trying to replicate; it is significant that there are no single memorable *monumental* interior spaces in any of his buildings compared with the sacred sense of the High Court interior at Chandigarh or Kahn's Assembly Hall at Dacca.

Sangath presents one of the most uplifting progressions of interlocking internal volumes of any of his projects, but almost at a domestic scale, as is the Husain-Doshi Gufa, whose residential component for the artist was adapted during construction. Premabhai Hall in Ahmedabad competes for the position of Doshi's single most awe-inspiring interior space, but fails to transcend its pragmatic function as a theatre. It is in the design of what Louis Kahn called 'outdoor rooms' that Doshi excels. The paved space between the Institute of Indology and its Phase II museum comes to mind, as do the open spaces under the School of Architecture and its covered pedestrian streets, the courts and external covered corridors of the Indian Institute of Management, the outdoor amphitheatre and water court protected by the office wings at Sangath, the inner courtyard at the Gandhi Labour Institute and its outer residential equivalent, the step well spine of the National Institute of Fashion Technology, or finally, the inner courts of the Bharat Diamond Bourse that all converge on a single protected common green full of water, grass and trees.

All of Doshi's latest projects, contemporary with the Diamond Bourse, are more obviously focused on 'outdoor rooms' or on hierarchical sequence than on the Modernist ideal of interior, ameliorative space as a constructed counterpoint to messy, unpredictable or dangerous nature. The Sardar Sarovar Narmada Nigam Administrative Building in Ahmedabad, begun in 1990, recalls the stylized step well at the NIFT elevated to 'a holy river, a cascading waterfall, a vast water body creating a deluge, a quiet place to meditate, sanctuaries for birds and animals'. The Yashwantrao Chavan Academy of Development Administration in Pune, is also dominated by open space, which the seven individual components of the complex surround in a roughly articulated U, with each component having its own central court. Sawai Gandharva Smarak nearby has an auditorium on the roof.

The 'amorphous' space about which he speaks is also not calculated to be the secular equivalent of a sacred predecessor as its Western component sought to be. The nearest metaphor that one can find for the soaring, hypostyle entry into the High Court at Chandigarh might be the Temple of Karnak, or a Gothic cathedral. The Arts and Crafts movement was the source of many Modernist tenets, the religious zeal of A. W. N. Pugin, and the promotion of Gothic architecture for England, distilled through the strict Anglican viewpoints of Ruskin and Morris, was later adopted in Germany through the efforts of Hermann Muthesius. The temple-like profile of Peter Behrens' AEG building in Berlin, which attempts to transform a sacrosanct image into the world of work, following soon after Charles Rennie Mackintosh's more literal translation of a Gothic cathedral in the library of the Glasgow School of Art, distills the trend from sacred to profane. The use of a Gothic cathedral on the cover of the Bauhaus Manifesto, in a woodcut by Lyonel Feininger, helps confirm the link.

In the many Hindu temples that Doshi consistently refers to as being inspirations in his work, such as those at Madurai and Tanjore, the spaces between the various skins, inside the walled compounds that Doshi calls the void spaces, assume more than the function of passages between the enclosed buildings. They are places of worship in their own right as part of the entire ritual.

STRUCTURE Structure, one of the most important definers of interior space in the Modernist canon, is converted in this exterior ethos to an articulating pattern on the walls surrounding the outdoor rooms that Doshi joins together. In much the same way the colonnades, porticoes, pilasters, stairs, and roof forms energize the edges of the open courts of an Indian temple. Doshi uses structure in an inverse way, to modulate, enliven and even to comment on the character of the outdoor spaces he creates. The most memorable examples, in no particular order, are the deep cuts in the bearing walls facing the interior court of the Gandhi Labour Institute, as well as the rank of barrel vaults that seem to levitate with magnificent presence above them. They also include the study of the architect's own residence in Ahmedabad, which presents monumental window jambs and an aedicule on the roof terrace above it to the garden which is as much a meditation space as the study is intended to be. The tartan grid that extends as exposed beams into the interior courts of IIM Bangalore, where *mashrabiya*-like windows overhang the perimeter wall and provide a staccato cornice line for those outdoor rooms also comes to mind. Projecting beams are used in a similar way at the School of Architecture at Ahmedabad, which knit the green space around the buildings with the external walls that surround it. These are only a few of the many examples that could be cited to describe Doshi's reversal of the expected use of structure in the Modernist sense. The way that such structures modulate light reinforces this inversion in his outdoor rooms.

LIGHT Louis Kahn had a quasi-mystical view of light, the moulder of interior space for the Modernists. His characterization of light as the primary life force, 'the giver of all presence', intensified its generative Modernist position, which remained intact during the transition from sacred to secular image described earlier. Light in the Gothic cathedral filtered through stained glass windows, representing the presence of God, following the visionary reference to it as such in Revelations 14:4. Its use by the early Modernists in the Farben works by Peter Behrens, the Deutscher Werkbund Exhibition in Cologne by Walter Gropius, or the Glass Pavilion at the same exhibition by Bruno Taut, for example, reinforces the sacred-secular connection in that transition. Kahn renewed and amplified that connection and his zealousness in maintaining that no room in any building should be without natural light, even if only to show 'how dark it really is', went beyond functional considerations and even at many times contradicted them. His feelings about the importance of natural light in interior spaces have been matched by few contemporary architects, with the exception perhaps of Tadao Ando, but Balkrishna Doshi has taken Kahn's sensibilities and attitude about natural light outside the building itself. This is most evident where outdoor rooms become streets, such as in the Indian Farmers' Fertilizer Co-operative in Kalol, north Gujarat of 1973, and the Life Insurance Corporation of Ahmedabad.

IIM Bangalore begins substantially to mark the fuller formulation of this strategy, most fully developed at Aranya, Indore in 1986. The streets of the Aranya project are literally an extension of the houses, which have parterres, balconies and open stairs with broad landings, which are all intended not to only enliven the street but, more importantly, as an outdoor extension of the house that is almost equal in square footage to the interior. Considering all of the variable combinations made possible for residents by the architect, it is remarkable that the streetscape also offers aesthetic unity with each permutation, as it does. The patterns of light and shadow come into play here: an outside component for each house along each street means that the view across it that those on the parterres will have, so that the possibility for various compositions becomes more than a refined game of scenography, it is the architectural background against which the residents of Aranya live their lives.

There are some who may feel that such subtle considerations as these are superficial in what is essentially a model of 'sites and service' self-help housing intended to provide a step up off the street for the very poor, who are the majority of Aranya's residents. When a similar criticism was put to Hassan Fathy about his model village at New Gourna, in which individually designed houses and services rather than just components were provided, he said, 'It isn't only the rich that deserve beauty, if anything the poor need it more than anyone.'

MATERIALITY Lastly, materiality is the most accurate way to trace how Doshi has adapted a Modernist credo to his regional purpose, retaining yet elevating older notions of honesty of expression. When Louis Kahn used brick with concrete to tie beams, he sent a clear message of his intention to expand the scope of the Modernist palette, intentionally limited to a post-industrial selection to affirm the break with historical periods or styles; but he, like Aalto, Scarpa and only a few others, drew the line at a less abstract recall, directly citing Roman precedents rather than historical reference twice removed, as in Mies van der Rohe's veiled reference to a Greek temple rendered in steel in the Farnsworth house. Kahn was on the brink of specificity, but it has remained for Doshi to take the next step. His willingness to retain the unsuitability of even the Kahnian concession to the past, which was just marginally acceptable under Modernist rules, is one of the most lasting contributions to the question of how to recognize the accumulated knowledge of a culture in the present. The concrete and brick walls of his earliest buildings were moss-covered and stain-streaked in less than ten years through no fault of his design. These materials simply do not do well in the hot humid climate of Gujarat. His persistent adaptation of new materials and old methods, such as the wire mesh, clay rope, thin concrete cover and ceramic chip finish used on the vaults of Sangath, clearly show his capacity for innovation. The vault, which recalls Kahn's work in appearance as well as in its drawing and so implies Kahn's tacit pact with the Modernist establishment, is also calculated to summon up images from the recesses of Indian history.

Nearing the final stage of a long and fruitful career, Doshi is now more productive and prolific than ever, but the majority of his buildings continue to be built in India. He also sees no need to participate in international competitions and so is denied that access to an international audience, unlike his contemporary Charles Correa, who won the RIBA Gold Medal in 1984. Yet his pragmatism and theoretical diplomacy, as well as his long involvement in education through the School of Architecture at Ahmedabad, may yet allow him to break free of the cycle of strictly local influence that seems to be the nemesis of architects who have attempted such regional interpretation elsewhere. The inexorable pressures of globalization will increasingly require architects to learn about and practice in cultures that are foreign to them and since most industrial growth is now taking place in the developing world, these are the societies that must be comprehended. Such pressure will inevitably lead to a heightened appreciation of Balkrishna Doshi's skill and the balancing of the sensibilities of East and West or North and South, depending on which labels for developed and developing nations are chosen. The aim of this study is to accelerate that appreciation because his contribution is so exceptional and valuable.

# Notes to the text

1 Balkrishna Doshi, 'Expressing an Architectural Identity: Bohra Houses of Gujarat,' *Mimar*, Jan.–Mar., 1986, p. 34.

2 *Ibid.*, p. 36.

3 Balkrishna Doshi, 'Memory, Association and Timelessness,' in *Architecture and Design,* Vol. V, No. 2, Jan.–Feb. 1989, p. 105.

4 Balkrishna Doshi, 'Between Notion and Reality', in *Architecture and Design*, Vol. V, No. 2, Jan.–Feb. 1989, p. 2.

5 Robert Venturi, 'Plus Ça Change'.

6 Balkrishna Doshi, *Architecture and Design*, Jan.–Feb. 1987, p. 60.

7 William Curtis, *Balkrishna Doshi: An Architecture for India*, New York 1988, p. 54.

8 Balkrishna Doshi, 'Buildings and Projects', *Architecture and Design,* Jan.–Feb. 1989, p. 47.

9 Louis Kahn, 'Talk at the Conclusion of the Waterloo Congress,' in *New Frontiers in Architecture,* Oscar Newman (ed.), Universe Books, New York, 1961, p. 212.

10 Larna Anagarika Govinda, *Psycho-cosmic Symbolism of the Buddhist Stupa*, Dharma Publishing, Berkeley, California 1976.

11 *Ibid.*, p. 5.

12 Anna Dallapiccola and Stephanie Zingelave Lallemant, *The Stupa: Its Religious, Historical and Architectural Significance*, Fran Stein Verlag, Wiesbaden, 1980.

13 *Ibid.*, p. 272.

14 George Michell, *The Architecture and Art of Southern India*, Cambridge University Press, 1995.

15 Balkrishna Doshi, 'The Revelation', unpublished, 1993.

16 Balkrishna Doshi, *Architecture and Design*, Jan.–Feb. 1989, p. 60.

17 Balkrishna Doshi, 'Buildings and Projects', *Architecture and Design*, Jan.–Feb. 1989.

# Chronology

**Residence for Mr Kantilal Banker**
*Ahmedabad, 1956–57*

**Premabhai Hall, first project**
*Ahmedabad, 1956*

**Ahmedabad Textile Industry's Research Association (ATIRA) and Physical Research Laboratory (PRL) Low Cost Housing**
*Ahmedabad, 1957–60*

Kasturbhai Lalbhai commissioned housing for ATIRA early in Doshi's career. This project was intended for service workers for the PRL, which the architect designed at the same time. Both projects are based on a simple repeated bay of parallel brick walls and vaults, with each unit opening out to a private court on one side and a continuous pedestrian way on the other. Light enters each unit through a clerestory between vault and wall.

**Residence for Mrs Pramila Chinubhai**
*Ahmedabad, 1959–60*

**Architect's Own House**
*Ahmedabad, 1959–61*

Located in Navrangpura, a suburb of Ahmedabad, Doshi's residence has been described as 'the first positive step toward translating Corbusier's lessons to fit the Indian context'. While using the Corbusian vocabulary of wide concrete fascias and deep setbacks, the house is sensitively oriented to sun and wind and has a non-compartmentalized, open plan that

Doshi House, Ahmedabad

allows for more flexible use of the interiors. Doshi wanted to recreate the shadow and proportions of Le Corbusier's Sarabhai house, and to use more polished surfaces.

**Science building for Gujarat University**
*Ahmedabad, 1959–62*

**Institute of Indology**
*Ahmedabad, 1957–62*

The first of Doshi's 'institutions', this is a combined museum and archive commissioned by L. D. Bhartiya Sanskriti Vidyamandir to house rare Jain manuscripts. The delicately balanced, temperature-controlled environment usually considered necessary in an archive was determined not to be advisable here because the

**Indian Farmers' Fertilizer Co-operative Township, Kalol, N.Gujarat**

manuscripts had been stored in a monastery and it was decided to retain conditions. The rectilinear plan positions the long side facing the prevailing breeze, behind a garden, which cools it. A hard court behind the building draws cool air though it by convection. The rare manuscript library is on the lower level, administration at the middle level and teaching rooms above. The reinforced concrete structure, grey slate floors and wide wood doors recall Le Corbusier, but the environmental considerations are characteristic of Doshi. (See pp. 28–37.)

**Hostel building and workshop for Gujarat University**
*Ahmedabad, 1958–63*

**Comprehensive school for Shreyas Foundation**
*Ahmedabad, 1960–66*

**ATIRA Guest House**
*Ahmedabad, 1961*

**Tagore Memorial Theatre**
*Ahmedabad, 1962–66*

**Township for Gujarat State Fertilizers Corporation**
*Baroda, 1964–69*

This is the first of a series of large corporate housing schemes, containing 1800 units grouped in several clusters that relate to company hierarchy. These clusters are organized inside a ring road, with cul-de-sac access roads serving each, stopping short of a central green. Brick and concrete are once again the principal materials. The straightforward grid used at ATIRA is refined here to provide covered passarelles, courts and housing in set, geometrically determined sequences, with a marked development of the use of bridges, balconies and overhangs as sculptural elements. (See pp. 48–59.)

**Library building for Gujarat University**
*Ahmedabad, 1963–65*

**Administrative office building for Gujarat State Fertilizers Corporation**
*Baroda, 1965–67*

**Bhandari House**
*New Delhi, 1966*

Built for Prema and Ranjit Bhandari in the verdant suburbs of the city, this concrete and brick house recalls Le Corbusier's Sarabhai Villa in materials and planning strategy. Based on a tartan grid that produces a rhythmic pattern of wide open archways and narrower, rectilinear doorway-sized bays, the two-storey residence has a monumental aspect, enhanced by a detached, triangular stair projecting at a 45 degree angle into the garden, recalling the Jantar Mantar observatory in the city. An arcade on both levels of the garden elevation provides shelter from the sun.

**Mohinaba Girls' High School
for Lalbhai Dalpatbhai Trust**
*Ahmedabad, 1966–68*

**School of Architecture**
*Ahmedabad, 1966–68 (First Phase)*

Doshi has not only designed the School of
Architecture, he helped to establish it, acted as its
first dean, and has served as a faculty member since
its inception. The architecture building, which is the
first phase of the Centre for Environmental Planning
and Technology (CEPT), is planned in parallel bays
along a north–south axis to allow maximum natural
light and ventilation and freedom of movement
through the studios and classrooms. Wide covered
walkways and stairs serve to link common spaces.
(See pp. 38–47.)

**Tagore Memorial Theatre (700 seats)
for Ahmedabad Municipal Corporation**
*Ahmedabad, 1967*

**Adinath Co-operative
Housing Society Limited**
*Pune, 1968*

**Rachana School**
*Ahmedabad, 1968–69*

**Staff housing for Ahmedabad
Education Society**
*Ahmedabad, 1965–67*

**Staff housing for Physical Research
Laboratory (PRL)**
*Ahmedabad, 1968–70*

**Students' hostel for Ahmedabad
Education Society**
*Ahmedabad, 1967–70*

**Regional office complex for
Central Bank of India**
*Ahmedabad, 1966–67*

**Township for the Electronics Corporation
of India (ECIL)**
*Hyderabad, 1968–71*

**Village rehabilitation scheme
for flood-affected area**
*Mandawa, 1968–70*

**Bhabha Atomic Research Centre (BARC),
Heavy Water Project (Kotah)**
*Bombay, 1969–73*

Nine variations of a housing type that provides
an open-plan living area, kitchen and bathroom with a
forecourt and a private court at the rear of each unit.
Ventilation shafts, which appear to be chimneys, funnel
cool air into each unit and sleeping terraces on the
roof, confirming Doshi's early awareness of vernacular
techniques of tempering the harsh local environment
in ways that make these houses, which range from 32
to 256 square metres, seem more spacious.

**TB Hospital (200 beds), ESIS Hospital**
*Ahmedabad, 1970*

**Master plan for Srinagar Lake Area
Development for Government of
Jammu and Kashmir (in association
with Joseph Allen Stein & Associates)**
*New Delhi, 1970–73*

**Indian Farmers' Fertilizer
Co-operative (IFFCO) Township**
*Kalol, Gujarat, 1970–73*

Combining and improving on the housing types
previously used in the Electronics Corporation of
India project of 1968–71 and Bhabha Atomic Research
Centre (BARC) of 1969–73, IFFCO also uses the
device of staggered siting of L-shaped units that are
paired and rotated. The front and rear courts used
previously are enhanced here, as are the sleeping
terraces, which are covered by pergolas. Staircases
also assume a more prominent, sculptural role here,
beginning a pattern that culminates at Indore.

**TB Hospital and Housing for
Gujarat Housing Board**
*Ahmedabad, 1970–72*

**Premabhai Hall**
*Ahmedabad, 1972 (final project)*

One of the most obvious instances of Corbusian
monumentality in Doshi's early career, Premabhai Hall
dominates the downtown area of Ahmedabad.
The reality of the required auditorium rake has been
used to great effect by the architect, as it has by other
functional expressionists such as James Stirling in the
Leicester Engineering Building, as a formal device that
allows the theatre to seem to soar up and over the open
square it defines. This concrete monolith that has
become the civic monument Doshi intended.

Premabhai Hall, Ahmedabad

**Campus Development for
Administrative Staff College of India**
*Hyderabad, 1971–73*

**National Assembly Building (project)**
*Kuwait, 1972*

Doshi was one of those invited to compete for
the commission to design this large governmental
complex, eventually won by Jorn Utzon. The area
along the coast of the Arabian Gulf, designated as the
site, is flat. The shoreline and the sea seem to blend
together and the Assembly complex was to be raised
up on a plinth base to make it more prominent against
the horizon. Doshi used principles of traditional local
architecture, such as the courtyard, *souk*, or market
street, and the Bedouin tent for layered shading, to
create a complex that was dignified and yet friendly in
scale. He also recognized other important landmarks
nearby, such as the Seif Palace. Utzon's winning
scheme played on many of these same themes, but
used the idea of the Bedouin tent in a more literal
way, with precast concrete folds sweeping up to create
a ceremonial entrance in front of a courtyard and a
pragmatic and inexpensive office complex behind it.

**Administrative, laboratory, dormitory and
ancillary facilities for International Crops
Research Institute for the Semi-Arid Tropics**
*Hyderabad, 1972–77*

**Research, development, planning
and information centre complex
for Indian Petrochemical Corporation Ltd**
*Baroda, 1972–75*

**Life Insurance Corporation (Bombay)**
*Ahmedabad, 1973–76*

**Administrative Building for
Indian Farmers' Fertilizer Co-operative**
*Kalol, 1973–76*

Covering 50-square metres, the complex is based on
the same principles used in Doshi's housing schemes:
pedestrian streets, forecourts, rear gardens, orientation
to attract the prevailing breeze and provide shade from
eastern and western sun, and the exaggeration of
necessary design elements, such as stairways, into
geometric forms that enhance imaginability and foster
a sense of community. As a 'collective', the complex
incorporates smaller units into larger ones to establish
a dense massing that is wider at the base than the top,
a difference accentuated by colour.

**Life Insurance Corporation of India,
middle- and low-income group housing**
*Hyderabad, 1974*

This project is similar in form to Kalol, but even more
dense because of severely restricted site conditions.
It uses triangular concrete stairways, providing access
to various sizes of flats stacked on many levels in the
same broad base and towering top configuration used
at Kalol. Doshi intended this as a framework that
could accommodate inevitable changes and it has
done that exceptionally well.

**Residence for Smt Sarojben
and Shri Vipinbhai Parikh**
*Ahmedabad, 1974*

**Urban renewal scheme
for redevelopment of Bhadra area**
*Ahmedabad, 1975–76*

**Extension to School of Architecture for
Ahmedabad Education Society**
*Ahmedabad, 1975–77*

**Administrative Staff College of India,
Computer Centre and library buildings**
*Hyderabad, 1976*

**Office and Council Chamber for
Ahmedabad Municipal Corporation**
*Ahmedabad, 1977*

**Shodhan Villa**
*Ahmedabad, 1977–79*

**Indian Institute of Management (IIM)**
*Bangalore, 1977–85*

Considered by the architect to be a benchmark in
his search for an appropriate modern expression of
traditional Indian architecture, the IIM Bangalore is
the result of an intense period of research into historical
prototypes. Doshi especially focused on Fatehpur Sikri
and the temple city of Madurai, which are each based
on a hierarchy of internal courtyards and colonnaded
covered passageways, and on purposely ambiguous,
rather than well defined, divisions between interior
and exterior space. 'Fatehpur Sikri,' Doshi determined,

is appreciated universally for…its spatial
organization. Here, one discovers solutions to

the now common problem of how to extend
buildings and yet relate them, how to ensure that
all the individual constituent parts of the complex
relate. This is achieved by adopting a system of
major corridors for movement along which activity
areas are disposed. And within the network of
corridors, the areas between the activity spaces
become courts for extended activities. These
courts [ensure] continuity of growth.

The variety of forms accommodated by this
system of courtyards and open corridor streets, without
discontinuity, is remarkable. This unity is strengthened
by the limited palette of materials used : concrete and
rough stone, blending with green landscape, sunlight,
shadow, and shade. (See pp. 60–71.)

**Museum Extension to Institute of Indology
for Lalbhai Dalpatbhai Trust**
*Ahmedabad, 1978–82*

**Senior Officers' Residences, US Embassy**
*New Delhi, 1978*

Similar in concept to the Bhandari residence of 1966,
these shallow-vaulted diplomatic quarters flank a quiet
street in the more verdant suburbs of Delhi. The clear
definition between concrete on horizontal surfaces and
brick in vertical bearing walls used at the Bhandari
residence is varied here by a washed terrazzo covering
which conveys a Mediterranean image and is
particularly effective in the strong Indian sunlight.
The vaults create deep shaded recesses to protect
living and dining rooms at ground-floor level and
lounges above. The profile of the vault recalls the
traditional *haveli* (mansion).

**Community Hall for Lions Club Society**
*Ahmedabad, 1977–79*

**Administrative Complex
for Madhya Pradesh Electricity Board (MPEB)**
*Jabalpur, 1979–87*

The boulders covering the hilly site for this large
public-sector organization prompted Doshi to consider
a crystalline geometry to unite the disparate parts of the
complex. The conceptual unit was the octagon derived
from a square, with corners cut at a 45 degree angle
to allow for circulation and service pods containing
offices, bathrooms and elevators attached to each of the
four straight sides. These service pods tower up above
the irregular octagons in the middle, which contain the
larger, more public spaces, and each cluster of pods and
central octagon rises or falls depending on the natural

contours beneath it, which have been left largely intact. Plaster finish containing the purple-brown stone chips from the local area, alternating with strips of dark brown polished granite, also help to resolve the building with the harsh landscape. The separation of 'served' and 'servant' spaces and repetitive geometry are reminiscent of Louis Kahn, particularly at the Erdmann Women's Dormitory at Bryn Mawr College. (See pp. 72–83.)

**Visual Arts Centre
for Leila and Purshottam Hutheesing Trust**
*Ahmedabad, 1975–79*

**Bhagwan Mahavir Memorial
for Bhagwan Mahavir Memorial Samiti**
*New Delhi, 1976–79*

**Sangath**
*Ahmedabad, 1979–81*

Of all the architect's projects, including his larger ones completed later in his career, Sangath remains his most memorable work and the clearest expression of his design philosophy. Carved into its slightly sloping site in urban Ahmedabad, it has been conceived as the physical expression of its Sanskrit name, which means 'moving together through participation'. It serves as an architectural office, research centre, school, place of contemplation, and built model of environmental consciousness. The penetration of the linear studio space into the ground protects the interior from the heat and gives the impression of complete unity with nature. This is even more obvious when approaching the vaulted, village-like cluster from the main entrance gate. A diagonal pathway, leading from the forecourt to the main entry and reception area, first leads left to give a perspective view of the ensemble, a classical strategy, then returns to the right past an outdoor amphitheatre, often used for extemporaneous discussions. The linear ranks of vaulted roofs have gaps between them for clerestory light and are faced with china mosaic chips. Water flows in a channel between them, cascading down in a waterfall near the front of the office. (See pp. 84–97.)

**Gandhi Labour Institute**
*Ahmedabad, 1980–84*

This centre for research and training in labour management and welfare is state-owned and consists of administrative facilities, classrooms, seminar rooms, a library, and accommodation for trainees. It was designed while Sangath, which is only one kilometre away, was in construction and there are obvious

parallels between the two that go beyond vaulted roofs. Essentially, the Gandhi Institute is the public equivalent of Sangath. While the connection to nature is achieved through courtyards, rather than burrowing into the ground, the environment is integral to the architecture. Rather than submerging the building, as at Sangath, Doshi raises it on a plinth in keeping with its public function, but it is still designed 'to relate an individual's centre to the physical and the intellectual world.' (See pp. 98–113.)

**Township for MPEB**
*Birsinghpur, 1982–85*

**Aranya Low-Cost Housing**
*Indore, 1983–86*

Doshi was commissioned by the Indore Development Authority to provide housing for the 'economically weaker sector', and the architect decided that some upper-income units should be integrated into the scheme to subsidize the lower-cost units. The target population was 40,000 on a 80-hectare site on the Mumbai–Agra highway, incorporating 6,500 plots, ranging between 35 and 475 square metres. Of these, 65 per cent were allocated for the very poor. It is a classic 'sites and services' project. Each lot had a fully serviced core containing a kitchen and bathroom and occupants can add to this as their means allow, selecting from a predetermined kit of parts. The idea was to provide components, but not define how they would be used, so the community could evolve as

*Vidyadhar Nagar (Jaipur New Town)*

traditional villages do. The general layout includes central commercial and office zones with streets radiating in non-linear pathways to six residential sub-zones. (See pp. 114–29.)

**Township for MPEB**
*Bodhghat, 1982–85*

**Kanoria Centre for Arts at CEPT premises
for Ahmedabad Education Society**
*Ahmedabad, 1984–86*

**Residence for Mr Kantilal Parikh**
*Nasik, 1984–86*

**Vidyadhar Nagar (Jaipur New Town)**
*1984–86*

This opportunity to design a new satellite town outside Jaipur allowed Doshi to expand the framework of his ideas beyond the housing solutions in his ECIL, IFFCO and GSFC corporate complexes, to include an entire community. He intended the plan 'to combine a traditional way of living with all present day facilities with provision for all the changes that may take place in the future'. His conviction, to combine traditional components of Indian civic architecture, such as the village square, the bazaar and the courtyard, with the

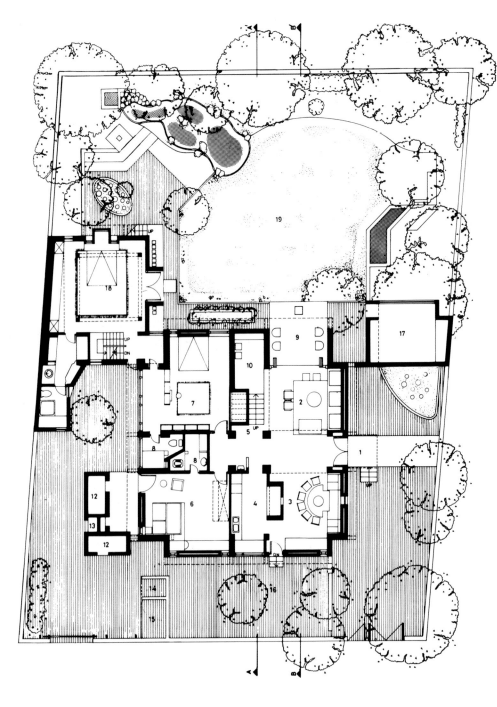

best contemporary infrastructure possible, led to an exhaustive study of traditional town-planning principles. This study focused on the old city of Jaipur built by Raja Jai Singh in 1727. It was based on the Vastu-Purusha mandala, an ordering system that attempts to correlate an ordered hierarchy with optimal orientation for shading and natural ventilation and division between public and private areas.

Doshi extended the environmental considerations of the mandala to accommodate the local climate of the Nahargadh hills, the terrain and utilize prevailing breezes. The 15,000 residential units were planned in high-density low-rise clusters grouped around linear open spaces and smaller courtyards. A main axial spine contains the majority of the office and commercial use buildings which are within walking distance of the residential areas. Water is a predominant feature in the open-space plan, representing the source of life.

### Extension to architect's own residence
*Ahmedabad, 1987–88*

Doshi viewed the design of his original residence in Navrangpura, a suburb of Ahmedabad, as one step in trying to translate Le Corbusier's ideas to fit the Indian context through more response to climate and context and a less rigid expression of functionality. He was deeply impressed by Le Corbusier's Sarabhai house, but not its rustic finishes. While he also uses brick and concrete, walls are plastered and floors are of polished slate. The original plan is a square divided into four quadrants, one for living, one for dining, the final two as parents' and children's bedrooms. The house takes up roughly half of a skewed rectangular lot, a garden the other half. This extension, thirty years after the original house was begun, is a library meditation room. It, too, is square in plan with columns in each corner supporting a mezzanine. It has selected views and a wide door out to the garden.

### Indian Institute of Management
*Lucknow, begun 1987*

### Maharashtra Institute of Development Administration (Yashwantrao Chavan Academy)
*Pune, 1987*

Established for people working on development schemes, the Academy teaches the proper administration of planned development. Doshi intends the environment, integrated into the U-shaped arrangement of faculty block, library, auditorium, classrooms, and dormitory blocks, to inspire renewal. He is designing courtyards, terraces and gardens in and around each of these elements so that the landscaping will weave through the entire complex. Covered corridors and pergolas will link them, with fountains at each end. This spine provides the continuity between components which each have a different footprint.

## Administrative complex
## for Sardar Sarovar Narmada Nigam, Ltd
*Ahmedabad, begun 1990*

The 1050-square-metre site for this administrative complex is in an institutional zone near the ring road at the western perimeter of Ahmedabad surrounded by low-rise housing, commercial and educational buildings. Sardar Sarovar oversees development along the Narmada River, including reforestation, and the design approach supports this environmental concern. Formed around a river-like channel, the complex includes semi-public discussion rooms, a library, auditorium, and dining area, all intended to boost public awareness of the work of the Nigam. For Doshi, the Narmada evoked many images 'of a holy river, a cascading waterfall, a deluge, a place to mediate, sanctuaries for birds and animals. Narmada's sacredness is a unique phenomenon. There is no river except the Ganges which has such power and houses so many ashrams.'

## Sawai Gandharva Smarka Auditorium
## and Cultural Complex
*Pune, 1991*

This institute for classical music contains classrooms, an indoor auditorium for performances, a rooftop amphitheatre and an administrative component that encircles the teaching and performance spaces. At 1800 square metres, it is compactly planned. An example of Doshi's more modest institutional projects, the transfer of the auditorium to the roof of this music school is notable.

## Husain-Doshi Gufa
*Ahmedabad, 1992–95*

Undeniably the most uncharacteristic and unorthodox of Doshi's buildings, the Gufa is a combination art gallery and residence to house the work of the Indian artist, M. F. Husain. The gallery, which is clearly expressionistic, relies on images of a primeval cave, chaitra, stupa, and female breast, formative and nurturing symbols that contrast sharply with the earlier rectilinear buildings also designed by Doshi for the campus of the Ahmedabad School of Architecture near the perimeter of the site. (See pp. 130–54.)

Tejal House, Ahmedabad

## National Institute of Fashion Technology
*Delhi, 1997*

Textiles are an important economic resource for India. Clothing design is a natural extension of it and this Institute was established to foster national pre-eminence in the field. The site chosen, adjacent to the Classical Dance Institute and Hauz Khas housing complex, was once a village with a lake in the centre. Doshi sought to recreate the spirit of that village in which 'the water body was sacred – because water was scarce…Several times a year, people from the surrounding villages gathered here to sing and select their future companions. Steps were built of bricks and took the shape of an irregular hill with several platforms, which were used for rituals…' Layered over this image is the idea of a bazaar, related to cloth and the theatrical quality of fashion. This suggested a sunken court, patterned after the step well of Adalaj, surrounded by platforms and galleries at various levels. This idea developed into two courts separated by a bridge, the first used as an entrance plaza related to reception and public functions, with student housing facing into the second, private court. Classrooms, laboratories and workshops are stacked in the two halves, facing into the courtyards, creating an introspective complex. Unfortunately, the step well concept is divisive because the steps are too high, discouraging interaction between the two halves of the scheme, rather than unifying the school, as the old step

well had done for the village that used to exist on the site. The bridge also divides, rather than unifies, cutting off the back half of the site from the activity in the front. The amphitheatre is symbolic only, and is not used, adding to the lack of activity beyond the bridge. Unlike other projects where the material palette is minimal and subdued, giving dignity to an institution, such as the Gandhi Labour Institute or the IIM Bangalore, the materials chosen here, such as reflective glass, contribute to the sense of fragmentation, making this one of the least successful of the architect's projects. (See pp. 156–71.)

## Bharat Diamond Bourse (BDB)
*Mumbai, 1998*

One of the largest projects by the Doshi atelier to date, the BDB is a symbol of India's growing financial status, its claim to the lucrative global diamond market previously controlled from Antwerp and Tel Aviv. Doshi's part-myth, part-revelation about the underground site conditions revealed during excavation show the extent of the architect's increasing reliance on instinct, intuition and emotion as important factors in his personal design approach layered over the learned rationalism he adopted at the beginning

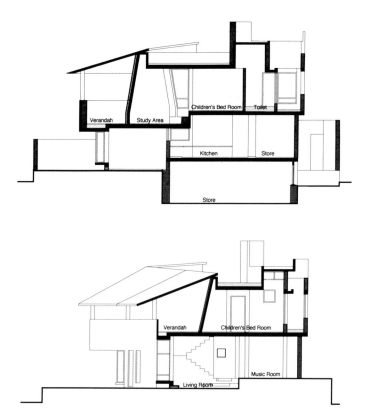

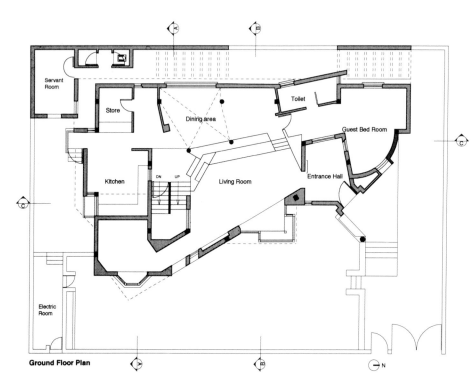

**Ground Floor Plan**

Tejal House, sections and ground floor plan

of his career. The BDB is a surprisingly strong
example of sustainable contemporary Indian building.
Doshi positions linear blocks to direct prevailing wind
through the huge complex and orients them for
maximum shade. (See pp. 172–185.)

### Tejal House
*1998*

Built in Vadodara for his daughter, this house contrasts
dramatically with Doshi's own orthogonal residence.
It uses a free-form geometry reminiscent of the
Husain-Doshi Gufa, derived from a similar ferrocement roof shell. The floors, of yellow Jaisalmer stone
polished to a mirror-like finish, fully glazed window
walls and built-in furniture confirm a new direction.
While Doshi used a Corbusian modular scale for
sectional profiles, and spatial volumes, the deliberate
juxtaposition of the column grid and wall structure,
use of the staircase as an extended living space, indirect
entry and spatial sequence, thorough concerns for
climatic controls and incorporating natural elements,
show the extent of Doshi's current departure from
those principles.

The playfulness of the curvilinear roof covering
the roof-deck verandah testifies to the freedom the
designer now enjoys. The inclined wall planes and
artistic composition of circles and stripes that puncture
the roof confirm Doshi's determination to 'unravel the
mystery of the mystical'.

### Khargar
*Mumbai, 1998*

Conceived as a satellite city of Mumbai, Khargar
represents an attempt to apply the concepts of
sustainability to the Indian context. The Vastu-Shilpa
Foundation has called the master plan an 'organic city'
because of its strong response to the environment and
emphasis on the conservation of natural resources. The
plan allows for flexibility and change. In keeping with
Doshi's outlook, the planners have sought answers as
much from an understanding of contemporary urban
development as from Indian tradition and heritage,
applying these criteria to four goals of livability,
accessibility, imaginability, and cultural appropriateness.

In adopting the approach of an 'organic' city, Doshi
was aware that this term is now controversial: many
planners disagree with the notion, popular in the
1960s, that an analogy can be drawn between
biological processes and urban growth. 'The basic
principle of the growth of cities,' Doshi maintains,

has remained constant: they grow by extension
and remodelling. Overlays of history are what give
a city its character, where time becomes visible.

The strong structures of historical, organically evolved cities, emerge out of the wisdom of the multitude, a logic which is always appropriate because it involves a collective thought, by which all factors are automatically considered.

The organic aspect of Khargar, then, is that it seeks to replicate the capacity of natural organisms to be self-sufficient entities; organisms are constantly evolving and yet complete at each stage of that evolution. Doshi realizes that the *tabula rasa* approach taken by Le Corbusier at Chandigarh was presumptuous and only succeeded because others, such as Doshi himself, helped to incorporate local elements into the plan. It is not possible to simulate the layers of history accumulated over time, but there are instances, such as the old city of Jaipur, which served as a model for Khargar, where planners have responded sensitively to culture and the dynamic aspect that Doshi seeks to harness, what he terms 'the architecture of life, of life systems'. He insists on placing each construction within the notion of an 'architecture of life', which he equates with the cosmos, saying that 'when one builds one simultaneously also inhabits, it is a question of layers, of various levels, in which nothing is built in isolation, but is part of a larger whole. The whole inhabits the part as much as the part inhabits the whole; the two are indivisible.'

The design criteria used to achieve this quality were contextuality, resource conservation, flexibility and incrementalilty, sustainability, financial viability, and a rational, iterative planning process. The key to realizing a majority of these criteria was a system of open spaces of various kinds, ranging from *maidans* that operate at the city wide level to the cul-de-sac at residential scale. These have been carefully defined and located as to type and usage, according to a hierarchy that begins with city centre squares, *maidans*, parks for the entire city, urban squares near important junctions, school playgrounds, linear green spaces along internal roads, including bicycle paths and small shops.

Another important aspect of the quality of life in Khargar is proximity to all facilities and major activity centres by fast, efficient public transportation networks and pedestrian links. The pedestrian paths widen at suitable junctions to accommodate local facilities and were visualized as an alternative transportation network, providing a quick, safe and healthy option for residents. The east–west orientation of residential streets responds to the local climate, minimizing solar radiation on the long elevations and permitting the prevailing winds to enter. This is only one instance of the way in which services are aligned with topographical lines and drainage patterns. Previous flooding originating in the hills to the west has been contained in channels which now water the public green spaces, saving the energy that would be used by pumping stations.

---

## Bandra-Kurla Complex
*Mumbai, 1998*

The complex will provide an alternative location for commercial activity that will relieve pressure on South Mumbai, providing a highly accessible, central location that will be even more convenient when a proposed east–west rail link is completed. It will include offices for Indian corporations and financial institutions as well as their international equivalents. Indian participants include ICICI, UTI, the National Stock Exchange, and NABARD.

In preparation for the design, the Vastu-Shilpa Foundation assessed the potential for the growth of such activity in Mumbai and undertook a background review of similar developments in other parts of the world. They also carried out a site analysis and established urban design guidelines that included road and transport networks and infrastructure. Detailed quantitative findings from these studies were essential to the establishment of a design brief for the IFBC. Nearly 35 hectares of the 166-hectare site were allocated to financial institutions and 18 hectares were set aside for a wholesale textile market.

Building heights in the complex were restricted to between 36 and 42 metres in this area because of the proximity of the airport, but this imposed uniformity was offset by varied topography and water features on or near the site, which enhance a park-like setting.

Doshi understood the need to provide services and what he terms 'agglomeration economies' adequately to support the financial institutions and corporations in the Centre. This led him to formulate six different plot typologies for the project: independent plots for large financial institutions; mixed use plots with offices, service and retail facilities; residential use; exclusively utility and service plots; parking facilities; and public space. The mixture of built form on these plot typologies was a critical design decision, especially the ratio of floor space to the net plot area. Holding capacity was another important potential linkages. Doshi wanted to avoid the cyclical character of such commercial centres elsewhere, or what he calls the 'dead after 6pm syndrome' and was careful to balance commercial and residential areas to avoid this, as well as to introduce activities into the institutional and commercial plots. It was determined that the financial institution clusters would be located along main roads to ensure accessibility with an adequate mix of plot sizes from 2500 square metres to 10,000 square metres to cater to both larger financial institutions and smaller business offices. The textile cluster was segregated from the financial institutions by a 45-metre-wide road, with maximum frontage along Bandra-Kurla Road. The residential units were distributed along the periphery to give them a separate identity, with the sloping topography and water incorporated as much as possible. Several residential areas were integrated with the office blocks to bring as much life into the IFBC as possible after office hours. Necessary services, such as the fire station, bus station, hospital, police station, telecommunication centre, post office and electric substation were grouped in one utility complex on 3.8 hectares of the site, with commercial and office space mixed with it to make the utility complex financially self-sufficient. A parking structure for 1350 cars is also located in this complex.

The highway and transport schemes for the IFBC were developed in tandem with the land-use proposals, with road hierarchy, pedestrian movement systems, bus systems, and location of parking garages the primary considerations. Arcades and underpasses have been provided whenever possible to encourage pedestrian use.

The Bandra-Kurla Complex is the first of its kind in India, and it was approached as an opportunity to introduce prototypical concepts and practices which would provide an 'Indian character', while also ensuring a financial centre that conforms to international standards. IFBC is intended as a model that will demonstrate how city governments can benefit from the commercial and economic development of areas under their jurisdiction, especially through the new infrastructure that such new complexes provide. Intelligent pricing policies at IFBC have generated significant financial surpluses. These have been used to set up an infrastructure fund which will help alleviate deficiencies in other parts of the Mumbai metropolitan region.

# Acknowledgments

The author would like to thank Balkrishna Doshi for his co-operation in the preparation of this book, and Yatin Pandya for all the help he provided. Ramkumar Supramanian and Anne Hong, students at the School of Architecture at the University of Southern California, assisted in the preparation of some of the drawings and I am grateful to them. Jo Newson was of invaluable assistance in helping me to formulate ideas at an early stage, as well as keeping me on track during difficult periods, as the work progressed. Her photographic contribution, especially of Chandigarh, is especially appreciated, helping to establish the character of the work. Jamie Camplin, at Thames and Hudson, has been unfailing in his support, despite unexpected delays and time pressures and has my gratitude for his patience, understanding and help.

Due to conflicts arising from the breakup of the partnership of Stein, Doshi and Bhalla, it has not always been possible to establish clear attributions of projects. I regret any omissions of credit that may have occurred. They were not intentional.

All photographs are by the author except for those listed below. Photographs by Joseph St Anne and John Paniker appear courtesy of the Aga Khan Award for Architecture.

**On the cover: (front)** Tim Bradley; **(back)** Joseph St Anne **2 (title page)** Jo Newson **4 (copyright page)** John Paniker **6–7, 11** (l), **13** (a) Jo Newson **13** (b), **14, 15** (b) Immanuel John Nicholas **15** (a) Jo Newson **16** Immanuel John Nicholas **17** (l), **19** (b) Jo Newson **20** (a) Ram Kumar **20** (b), **21** (a) Immanuel John Nicholas **25** (r), **30** (l), **31, 32** (a, bl) Jo Newson **32** (br) Immanuel John Nicholas **34, 37** Jo Newson **39** Immanuel John Nicholas **40, 41** (a), **44** Ram Kumar **48–59** Vastu-Shilpa Foundation **60** Immanuel John Nicholas **61** Jo Newson **62** (a) Immanuel John Nicholas **62** (b), **63** Jo Newson **66–67, 68** (b) B. V. Doshi **68** (a), **69–70** Yatin Pandya **71** B. V. Doshi **72–73** Ram Kumar **74** Yatin Pandya **75** Ram Kumar **76–77** Joseph St Anne **78–79** Ram Kumar **80** Yatin Pandya **81** Ram Kumar **82–85** Joseph St Anne **86** (a) B. V. Doshi, courtesy AKAA **87** Anne Hong **88–89** (a) Joseph St Anne **89** (b) Immanuel John Nicholas **91** Anne Hong **92** (r) Immanuel John Nicholas **92** (l), **93–95** (b) Joseph St Anne **95** (a) B. V. Doshi **96** Jo Newson **97** Joseph St Anne **98–99** Jo Newson **100** Dinesh Mehta **101** Anne Hong **102–7** Jo Newson **108** Anne Hong **109–12** Jo Newson **113** Anne Hong **114** Yatin Pandya **115** John Paniker **116–17** B. V. Doshi **118** (l) Immanuel John Nicholas; (r) Yatin Pandya **119** (a) John Paniker; (b) Yatin Pandya **122** (a) B. V. Doshi; (b) Yatin Pandya **123** (a) Yatin Pandya; (b) John Paniker **124–25** B. V. Doshi **126** (l) Yatin Pandya; (r) John Paniker **127** Yatin Pandya **129** B. V. Doshi **130** Immanuel John Nicholas **132–33** D. Shaw Axiom **134** Immanuel John Nicholas **136** Tim Bradley **137** Anne Hong **138–39** Tim Bradley **140** Anne Hong **141** John Paniker **145** (b), **147, 148** (a) Ram Kumar **149** John Paniker **152–53** Ram Kumar **158–59** B. V. Doshi **161, 162** (a) Immanuel John Nicholas **162** (b) Vastu-Shilpa Foundation **163** Hassan Udin Khan **165** (a) Immanuel John Nicholas **167** B. V. Doshi **168–69** Jo Newson **171** Steven Goldberg **172** B. V. Doshi **173** Ram Kumar **174–75** B. V. Doshi **176** Ram Kumar **177–80** B. V. Doshi **195** Joseph St John **196, 198–200** Vastu-Shilpa Foundation **197** Joseph St John **201** Yatin Pandya **202** Vastu-Shilpa Foundation

# Bibliography

### WRITINGS BY BALKRISHNA DOSHI

'Mons. Le Corbusier', *Marg*, Bombay, 1953

'Main Structure Concept', in *Landscape*, USA, 1963, pp. 17–20

'Concept of Main Structure', with Christopher Alexander, *Landscape*, Vol. 13, No. 2, 1965

'Indian Architecture and its Criticisms', Cultural Forum, Ministry of Scientific Research and Culture, Government of India, 1965

'Architecture for Time and Change – A System, *Kenchiku Bunka*, Japan, January 1967

'The Proliferating City and Communal Life: India', in *Ekistics*, 1968, pp. 67–69

'Sanctuary for the Arts', *Indian Express*, 27 March, 1969

'Problems of Ahmedabad', Gujarat Chamber of Commerce and Industry, *Ahmedabad Bulletin*, Vol. 16, No. 1, January 1971

'The Unfolding of an Architect', *Global Architecture* (special issue), Japan, 1973

'Louis I. Kahn in India', *Architecture and Urbanism*, Japan, March 1975

'Ahmedabad – Blend of Old and New', *The Times of India*, 1977

'The Impetus to Build', interview with William Marlin, *Christian Science Monitor*, Boston, 16 June 1977

*Integrated Rural Development Plan for Village Chharodi*, Vastu-Shilpa Foundation, 1979

*Know Your City: Ahmedabad Information Sheets*, Vastu-Shilpa Foundation, 1980

Concluding remarks at the Amman Seminar, Aga Khan Award for Architecture, Jordan, 1980, pp. 135–37

'Identity in Architecture: Contemporary Pressures and Traditions in India', in *Architectural Association Quarterly*, London, October 1981

'Louis Kahn in India', in *Architectural Association Quarterly*, 1981

'Le Corbusier – Acrobat of Architecture', *Architecture and Design*, 1981, pp 54–59

'Centre for Environmental Planning and Technology, Ahmedabad, India', in *Mimar*, Cambridge, Massachusetts, Oct./Dec., 1981

'Architecture and Attitudes', *Akriti*, on the 24th Convention of National Association of Students of Architecture, 1982, pp. 4–6

*Low-Cost Housing, Phase I and II*, Vastu-Shilpa Foundation, 1983

*East Ahmedabad Development Plan: A Conceptual Plan Strategy*, Vastu-Shilpa Foundation, 1984

*Low-Cost Housing, Indore*, Vastu-Shilpa Foundation, 1984

'Low-Cost Housing Township at Indore', *Open House International*, 1984, pp. 34–44

'Le Corbusier – Acrobat of Architecture', interview by Carmen Kagal in *The Architecture of India*, October 1986, pp. 204–14

'Architecture for India – A Personal Interpretation', in *Journal of International Laboratory of Architecture and Urban Design*, Siena, Italy, 1987

'Between Notion and Reality', *Reflection*, published at the 1987 Indian Institute of Architecture Convention, p. 187

'Learning from Old Jaipur', with Muktirajsinhji Chauhan, *Journal of the Indian Institute of Architects*, 1987, pp. 30–35

'Architectural Education, Allied Disciplines and the Community', in *Journal of Indian Institute of Architects*, September 1988

'Le Corbusier – My Guru', interview with Mina Singh in *Inside/Outside*, 1988, pp. 148–51

'A Rediscovery', interview with Sarayu Ahuja, *Indian Architect*, 1988, pp. 4–11

'Balkrishna V. Doshi', in *Architecture and Design*, New Delhi, Jan./Feb. 1989

'Between Notion and Reality', in *Indian Institute of Architects Journal*, Bombay, March 1989

'Planning for a Community – Vidyadhar Nagar', in *International Social Science Journal*, August 1990

**PAPERS**

'Regionality', World Design Conference, Tokyo, 1960

'Environment', International Design Conference, Aspen, Colorado, 1962

'Proliferating Unplanned Cities and Their Relation to Religion, Architecture and the Visual Arts',
Congress on Religion, Architecture and the Visual Arts, USA, September 1967

'Self Sufficiency and Generative Centres', International Design Conference, Aspen, Colorado, June 1969. Published in *Ekistics*, 1970, p. 209–11

'Human Stake in Environmental Improvement', UN Seminar on Impact of Urbanization on Man's Environment, USA, June 1970. Published in *Ekistics*, 1970, p. 424–26

'Rural Housing', Symposium on Rural Development by Agency for International Development at Georgia Institute of Technology, 1975

*Habitat Bill of Rights*, with Jose Louis Sert, Moshe Safdie and Nadar Ardalan, for the Government of Iran for submission to the UN Conference on Habitat, 1976

'Ahmedabad – the Historic City', for the *Encyclopedia of Architecture*, Urban Planning, Harvard University, 1977

'Limits to City Growth', Cairo Symposium, 1978

'Architectural, Cultural, Social, and Economic Attitudes in India Today', International Conference on Architecture and Planning sponsored by Forum, Architecture Communications Territoire at Lausanne, 1979

'General Education in India: A Search for Relevance', International Symposium on the Contents of General Education During the Course of the Coming Decades, UNESCO, Paris, 1979

'Spatial Hierarchies and the Role of Small and Medium Towns', 29th Annual Town and Country Planning Seminar at Gandhinagar Gujarat, 1981

'Ahmedabad – Past, Present and Future', symposium organized by Ahmedabad Citizens' Council, 1984

**TALKS**

'Architecture', All India Radio, December 1960

'Rural Housing', All India Radio, 10 March, 1970

'Search for a Cultural Continuum in Architecture and Community Planning', keynote address at the Indo-US Subcommission on Education and Cultural Seminar on Architecture and Cultural Planning, published 1981, pp. 37–39

'Urbanisation and Cultural Continuity', keynote address at the Indian Institute of Architects Convention, Bombay, 1984

'Some Notes Towards a Holistic Habitat: Professional and Educational Implications', keynote address at the National Workshop on Architectural Education, sponsored by the Council of Architecture at the School of Architecture, CEPT, Ahmedabad, 1987

'Bharatiya Ghar (Indian Home)', Vatsal Nidhi at Alwar, 1987

'The Rest of Our Lives', International Design Conference Bulletin, Aspen, Colorado, 1969, p. 42–45, published in *Ekistics*, March 1970

**ON BALKRISHNA DOSHI**

Moro, P., 'Premabhai Hall, Ahmedabad', in *Architectural Design*, London, September 1960

Aoki, S., 'Impression of Doshi and His Works', in *Kindai Kenchiku*, Tokyo, June 1964

Blake, P., 'Architecture for a Time of Change', in *Architectural Forum*, New York, December 1965

Kultermann, Udo, *New Architecture in the World*, New York, 1965

'India Today', special issue of *Architectural Review*, London, December 1971

'Balkrishna Doshi', in *Architectural Forum*, New York, May 1973

'Eminent Architects', *The Illustrated Weekly of India*, 1973, p. 35

Ventin, C.A., 'Canada – Arquitectura education y hospitaliria', *Escuela del Sagrado Corazon*, 1976, p. 29

Marlin, William, 'Designing Shady New Buildings for India', in *Christian Science Monitor*, Boston, 16 June 1977

De Carlo, Giancarlo, 'Designing in India between Contemporary Pressures and Tradition', *Spazio-e-Societa*, Milan, September 1978, pp. 5–40

'Talking of Balkrishna Doshi', *Spazio-e-Societa*, 1979, pp. 3–4

Rao, Meenakshi, 'The Best House', *Inside/Outside*, 1979, pp 8–17

'Arquitectura en la India – Doshi', *Summarios*, Argentina, June 1979, pp. 56–79

Kultermann, Udo, 'Balkrishna Doshi, Ahmedabad (Indien)', *Architekten der Dritten Welt*, Paris, 1980

'Familiar Patterns', in *Building Design*, London, 5 December 1980

Marlin, William, 'Through the Doors of Doshi', *Inland Architect*, Chicago, April 1981, pp. 4–23

Pettruccioli, Attilio, 'The Institutions of Man', *Spazio-e-Societa*, March 1983, pp. 64–73

'The Office of an Architect who Holds to Traditional Values', *The American Institute of Architecture,* 1983, p 169

'Sangath – The Doshi Office in Ahmedabad', in *Architecture d'aujourd'hui*, Paris, September 1983

Sen, Dr Geeti, 'Sangath, B. V. Doshi's Unique Office Complex', *Inside/Outside*, Bombay, Oct./Nov., 1983, pp. 24–37
———, 'Subterranean Vaults', in *Inside/Outside*, Bombay, Oct./Nov., 1983

'Doshi in Bangalore', *Sunday Herald*, Sunday edition of *Deccan Herald*, Bangalore, September 25, 1983

Petrilli, Amedeo, 'A City Made up of Many Villages', *Spazio-e-Societa*, March 1984

Rybczynski, Witold, 'The Last Outpost', in *Architects' Journal*, London, October 1984

Works mentioned in *Architecture+Design*, inaugural issue, Nov./Dec. 1984, pp. 28–29

Interview, *The Fifth Column*, Canadian students' journal of architecture, 1985, pp. 32–36

Petruccioli, Attilio, 'The Institutions of Man', in *Techniques et Architecture*, Paris, 1985

'Vidyadhar Nagar, Jaipur', *Journal of the Indian Institute of Architects*, Sep., Dec. (Issues 3 and 4), 1987, pp. 8–13

Curtis, William, *Balkrishna Doshi: An Architecture for India*, New York 1988

Chauhan, Muktirajsinhji, et al, 'Balkrishna V. Doshi: the Architect as Oracle', in *Architecture and Design*, New Delhi, Sept./Oct. 1993

# Index

Page numbers in *italics* indicate illustrations.